A PLAIN PINE BOX

A PLAIN PINE BOX

A Return to Simple Jewish Funerals
and
Eternal Traditions

by
Rabbi Arnold M. Goodman

KTAV PUBLISHING HOUSE, INC.
NEW YORK

Library of Congress Cataloging in Publication Data

Goodman, Arnold M
  A plain pine box.

  Includes bibliographical references.
  1. Funeral rites and ceremonies, Jewish—Minnesota—
Minneapolis. 2. Chevra Kevod Hamet, Minneapolis.
3. Jews in Minneapolis. I. Title.
BM712.G64   296.4'45   80-28424
ISBN 0-87068-895-2   AACR1

Manufactured in the United States of America

This book is dedicated to the men and women of the Adath Jeshurun Chevra Kevod Hamet. Their willingness to give of themselves to honor the dead and to strengthen the living has given new life to ancient customs.

When Rabbi Bunam lay dying, his wife burst into tears. He said, "What are you crying for? My whole life was only that I might learn to die."

—*Martin Buber*
Tales of the Hasidim:
Later Masters, p. 268.

Contents

Acknowledgments

I wish to thank the following for permission to use certain copyrighted material:

The Jewish Publication Society of America for the courtesy of quoting copyrighted passages in *Community and Polity* by Daniel Elazar.

Adath Jeshurun Congregation, Minneapolis, Minnesota, for permission to reproduce forms found in the Appendices.

Foreword

"I like the idea of leaving life as simply as I came. I came with blood, I do not want to leave with formaldehyde. I came naked, I do not need to leave with a polyester dress. I came alone, people anticipating my birth, I leave alone and hope people will share in my death."[1]

This book is the story of a group of people, members of Minneapolis's Adath Jeshurun Congregation, who, in their decision to bury the dead simply and "without formaldehyde," demonstrated a willingness to accept responsibility for their own lives. In so doing, they had an impact upon the synagogue, the Jewish community, and the general community. The impetus to return to, and to embrace, traditional Jewish burial and mourning practices demonstrates the ongoing relevance of a ritual system which spans centuries— even millennia.

The focal point for Jewish life has always been the synagogue. The values prevalent in the general society within which the synagogue found itself, however, have always had an effect, at times greater, at times lesser, upon this authentic Jewish institution. This historical process is reflected in the Yiddish proverb, "Wie es Krisstelt zich, azei Yiddelt es zich" (As it goes with Christians, so goes it with Jews). In the United States this process has helped to shape the synagogue into a reflection of American capitalist society.

---

1. Unpublished paper by a student at College of St. Catherine, St. Paul, Minnesota.

Jews, in fact, perhaps more than other groups, have integrated the economic, social, and political values of American capitalism. American Jews have invested themselves, physically and emotionally, as well as financially, in the stability, viability, and continuity of American capitalism.

Responding to and handling the dead is one area in which American values have come to predominate in Jewish society at the expense of traditional Jewish values. The twentieth century has witnessed an expansion of the American funeral industry, which realizes over $4 billion annually. Lavish funeral homes, expensive caskets fabricated out of metals and lined with costly materials, hermetically sealed grave liners, often personalized with the deceased's name on the lid, embalming procedures, cosmetizing, and even special clothes and shoes for the deceased's final dressing, are all part of the American response to death. The cost is further increased by the grave cost, the price of grave opening and closing, and perpetual care. American free enterprise in all of its glory is reflected in the American tradition of serving the dead and their families. The funeral industry is big business. It has succeeded, in large part, because people prefer not to confront death or deal with it. The preference of Americans to be "death-denying" has spawned institutions that stand between the living and the dead.

The commercialization and professionalization of handling death have removed most of us from really dealing with it. Customs of the past, in which families and friends would assume responsibility for preparing the dead for burial, for making arrangements with—and for—the family, for fabricating coffins and burial garments, have all but disappeared. America's increased affluence, plus a variety of death benefits, have made it possible to pay others to do for people what people formerly did for themselves and for others.

As people became further and further removed from handling death, a mystique inevitably came to surround it.

The more mysterious death became, the more essential that it be left to the professional—in this case, the funeral director.

The funeral industry, like any other, reflects a cross-section of self-interests. Given the large sums of money to be made, it was natural that for some funeral homes profits came to transcend the needs—and the rights—of the consumer. Instances of families being "sold" on more expensive caskets, of agreeing to services not always necessary, of being told that certain practices or items were required by law, when in fact they were not, are some of the more common abuses alleged by families who felt they were "sold" more than was necessary.

During the past two decades, consumer responses to abuses, alleged and real, were reflected in books, such as Jessica Mitford's *The High Cost of Dying,* and in the formation of memorial societies. The latter have as their goal prearranged funerals which, while inexpensive, are nonetheless dignified. For whatever reason, critics of the funeral industry who were interested in economic relief did not meet with widespread success in modifying its practices.

In September 1975, the Federal Trade Commission issued a preliminary report focusing on the abuses, both alleged and proven, of the funeral industry. Central to the report was the contention that a bereaved family is in a poor bargaining position as a consumer, having to negotiate an economic arrangement when the dead are literally before them. The FTC report cited practices and procedures which were disturbing not only on the "consumerism" level, but also on the Jewish level.

A reading of the FTC report makes it obvious that Jewish funeral processes are not substantially different from those of the general American society. Jews, too, opt for lavish funerals, expensive caskets, and a variety of cosmetic procedures to prepare the body for burial. The insight of the

Talmud that "there is no dominion on the day of death" is all but disregarded as American Jews reflect the values of the general society.

Jews have become like everyone else, not only in embracing the expensive funeral in the well-appointed mortuary, but also in relegating much of the preparatory process to others. Other than the functioning of small Chevrot Kadisha (Sacred Societies)—generally comprising but a handful of older people who perform the ritual purification—there is virtually no direct involvement by friends or family in the process of preparing the deceased. The "hands-on" dimension has all but disappeared as more and more responsibility is relegated to the funeral director.

The phenomenon of delegating responsibility to others, to have professionals serve as surrogates, is not only characteristic of our response to death. In virtually all areas of Jewish life, major tasks have been relegated to others who assume responsibilities as professionals or paid staff. The affluence of the Jewish community and its willingness to pay for services rendered, has given rise to the term "checkbook Judaism." The vast synagogue complexes built in post–World War II Jewish suburbia reflect both the abdication of direct involvement in Jewish affairs and the ability to pay for others to serve as our surrogates.

The second generation in suburbia came of age in the 1960s. Activism suddenly took on great appeal. Young people protested the passivity which they saw and began to demand a role in determining their destiny and that of their community. The rebellion against the large, well-appointed synagogue-temple was, for dedicated Jewish youth, expressed in the Havura movement, in campus kosher dining clubs, in Jewish communes.

In 1975–76, the Adath Jeshurun Congregation, Minnesota's oldest Conservative synagogue, began to respond to a twofold challenge: the restoration of tradition to Jewish funeral practices and the criticisms of the activist movement. The two were interrelated because a return to traditional funeral practice necessarily meant people's involvement in the process of caring for the dead and strengthening the mourner.

We knew that Jews were willing to tithe their money. Would they also tithe their time and their talents? There had generally been but limited demands upon people to make this kind of contribution. Professionals, by and large, were pleased to have volunteers out of the way, and the public was usually delighted to have others do for them.

The reluctance to make demands upon congregants may account for the boredom projected by many congregations and for their diminishing appeal to many dedicated young people. While a large segment of our community is satisfied with things as they are, many people refuse to tolerate a situation which makes passivity a fashionable norm. The latter group often finds its way into groups, communes, and societies far removed from Jewish life.

The Adath Jeshurun Congregation's Chevra Kevod Hamet (lit. Society to Honor the Dead) urges people to become involved in areas of their own competence. The Chevra recognizes that the continuation of every human institution is ultimately based on its ability to serve its people. The Chevra posits that the best way to serve people is to provide them with the knowledge, the inspiration, and the means to help themselves.

Intrinsic to this entire process is a perception of the synagogue as a community which provides for the needs of its members without excessive cost. The Chevra recommended, and the congregation board approved, a model whereby a traditional funeral would be provided free of charge to all congregation members. It was hoped that a commitment of such magnitude would impress upon the congregation's membership the seriousness with which the synagogue viewed its responsibility to its members and that of synagogue members to one another. It was obvious that the congregation's plan could work only if many people were willing to discharge a variety of functions.

This was an open challenge to the activist strain in our midst. Was there really sufficient commitment to maintain a project in which people involved themselves with the dead? There were, in addition, other issues and concerns.

1. Was it possible for our synagogue—indeed any synagogue—to set up a model of dealing with death and dying in which traditional values could be followed?
2. Would people help people simply for the sake of a *mitzva* (a commandment or good deed)?
3. Would people be able to transcend the denial of their own mortality and confront death with its implications of their own ultimate fate?
4. What, if anything, was relevant to us from the "memorial society" model?
5. Could we call for an appraisal of the community's single Jewish funeral home without falling into the trap of "economic consumerism"?[2]
6. Was it valid or appropriate for a single synagogue to initiate a project which sought to solve a community problem? Was it right for a single synagogue to take any action which might affect the entire community?
7. What spinoff, if any, would there be from the Chevra model of maximum involvement to other areas of synagogue activity? Was the handling of the dead *sui generis*—unique unto itself?

We quickly learned that a significant number of people

---

2. In February 1980, a second Jewish owned funeral home opened in Minneapolis.

were prepared to involve themselves in caring for the dead and strengthening the living, thereby fulfilling the *mitzva* of *kevod hamet* (honoring the dead). It was also apparent that the FTC allegations touched the feelings of many people. There was unhappiness with the sense of detachment built into the funeral industry, as well as with the high costs involved.

The Chevra began its work in response to a sermon preached on the first day of Rosh Hashana (the Jewish New Year) 5736 (1975). The assumption of the pulpit message was that our departure from tradition has not served us well.

The pages that follow contain the story of the Chevra Kevod Hamet: its origin, its membership, its successes, and its problems. The chronicle of the Chevra is a story of how synagogues function, of synagogue-federation relationships, of the potential for rabbinic-lay colleagueship.

The story of the Chevra is also a story of vested interests, of fear of the unknown, of the role of leadership, and of the use and abuse of the mass media. It is, perhaps most importantly, a statement of how Jewish tradition can be revitalized and made into a force in the life of the contemporary Jew.

It is left for the reader to decide whether the Chevra is within the mainstream of Jewish life or merely a tributary.

Minneapolis, Minnesota
Elul 5740
August 1980

1

The Chevra Kevod Hamet Is Born

They had traveled to Israel together. The woman, in her sixties, showed the effects of a long bout with illness. The man, a generation younger, was aggressive and competent; he was the chairperson of the congregation's newly announced Chevra Kevod Hamet.

"Will you really take care of me?" she asked.

"Of course," he replied.

Within six months she died. Her children, confronting the reality of her death, were overwhelmed. At that moment of bereavement, they had no idea of how to proceed. Their painful confusion ended when they realized that their mother had requested that she be buried through the Chevra. Arrangements for her burial were made easily and naturally.

He kept the promise: she was taken care of! Many of the people who traveled with her to Israel shared in the process in which she was ritually washed, carefully dressed in shrouds and placed in the coffin, borne to the grave, and then gently covered with a blanket of earth.

*　　*　　*　　*　　*　　*　　*　　*

They were a childless couple from the "old country." The call came at 4:30 in the morning. The nurse's tone was urgent. "Mr. —— has just died and his wife is all alone. She has no idea of what to do. Will you come?" I arrived at the hospital as dawn was breaking.

"Yes," she said, "I want the Chevra for him. This is the way we did it in Europe."

Within minutes the funeral home had been notified. The two of us remained with the body as *shomrim* (guardians) until the undertaker arrived. I drove her home and placed a call to the *chaver* (counselor) on duty. The *chaverim* team was there shortly; their presence brought support, morale, and care.

*   *   *   *   *   *   *   *

His death was peaceful—as befitted a man over ninety who was a respected teacher and scholar. His students sat as *shomrim* with the body. The members of the Chevra Kadisha regarded it as a signal honor to wash and purify his body; they knew they would be the last human beings to touch him.

At the cemetery, dozens of men and women, adults and teenagers, formed themselves into a line to shovel earth into his grave. It was appropriate, they knew, to fulfill the *mitzva* of burying the dead. With love they covered him with a blanket of earth.

*   *   *   *   *   *   *   *

From its inception on Rosh Hashana, 5737 (September 1976), the Chevra Kevod Hamet of the Adath Jeshurun Congregation in Minneapolis has been both a source of comfort to bereaved families and the subject of heated controversy within the funeral industry and elsewhere. Mourners have praised the dedication of the Chevra and its volunteers; the funeral industry has condemned it. The rabbinate has been divided in its response; the Minneapolis Jewish community has been perplexed as it seeks to assess the meaning of this novel congregational program. Media coverage has been enthusiastic, with ABC making the Chevra the subject of a national TV documentary entitled *A Plain Pine Box.*

The story of the Chevra Kevod Hamet is also the story of vested interests. The challenge of the Chevra inspired people to become autonomous as they began to perceive themselves as competent to take care of themselves. The Chevra is also a model of how Halacha (Jewish law) can be viable for a twentieth-century Jewish community living in a materialistic and technologically advanced society.

The Chevra Kevod Hamet, like Topsy, "just growed." It began with the sermon on the first day of Rosh Hashana, 5736. The subject was the impact of American values upon Jewish tradition, with one illustration being the funeral and mourning practices of American Jewry.

Interest in this subject was motivated by the publication of a Federal Trade Commission memo on funeral practices. The document criticized the funeral industry for a variety of abuses, such as embalming corpses without permission, misleading families as to the legal necessity of embalming, concealing the availability of less expensive caskets, and discouraging selection of particular merchandise.

A quarter-century of experience in the rabbinate confirmed that these abuses were not limited to Gentile-owned mortuaries. Embalming, expensive caskets, vaults, and the overall profit motive to which the FTC was reacting were characteristic also of Jewish-owned mortuaries. As Jews became more and more acculturated, differences between Jewish-owned and Gentile-owned funeral homes became blurred.

As I studied the FTC report, two thoughts came to mind. Firstly, there was a Jewish model for responding to death and bereavement. The Halacha was very clear and concise, both as to what was expected of a Jew who was bereaved and how a dead body was to be treated. Had the abandonment of Halacha served us well, or would it be well to take another look at the validity of the Halachic model?

Secondly, the rabbinate was in a very precarious situation; any change in the pattern of handling funerals would be seen, at best, as an admission of poor judgment, and at worst, as negligence. Perhaps it was wiser not to challenge the status quo. Ambivalence was put to an end by the famous text in the Talmud describing the process by which democratization became the norm in traditional Jewish funerals.

> Formerly, they were wont to bring out the rich for burial on a *dargesh* [a tall, stately bed, ornamented and covered with rich coverlets] and the poor on a plain bier, and the poor felt shamed; they instituted, therefore, that all should be brought out on a plain bier, out of deference for the poor. . . .
>
> Formerly, the expense of taking the dead out to burial fell harder on his near-of-kin than his death, so that the dead man's near-of-kin abandoned him and fled, until at last Rabbin Gamaliel came forward and, disregarding his own station, commanded that he be buried in linen [rather than expensive woolen] vestments. Thereafter people followed his lead to be buried in linen vestments.
>
> Said Rabbi Papa, "and nowadays all the world follows the practice of burial in a paltry shroud that costs but a zuz."[1]

As a spiritual descendant of Rabbi Gamaliel, I had little choice but to raise the issue before the congregation and to urge the formation of a committee to study the feasibility of creating an Adath Jeshurun funeral plan. Jules Levin, congregation president, sympathized with this request and permitted me to issue from the pulpit a call for the committee. The process was thus begun even before the sermon.

The response to the sermon was overwhelming. Many people had negative experiences when arranging for the funeral of a loved one. Not surprisingly, over twenty people came forward to volunteer for the study committee. The chairmanship was assumed by a vice-president of the congregation, who was professionally a clinical psychologist.

---

1. Tractate *Moed Katan* of the Babylonian Talmud (Soncino trans.), p. 27b.

In a letter notifying the volunteers of the committee's first meeting, the chairman requested that everyone prepare a brief statement on "Why I joined the committee." Many of the responses focused on the issues raised by the FTC: overselling when vulnerable, nonavailability of a less expensive coffin, a bill which somehow grew and grew, and so on. Others expressed dismay that the Jewish-owned funeral home showed little real awareness of—or perhaps what was worse, little concern for—Halacha. One person in particular complained that her wish to bury her mother in a simple wood box had brought forth the retort: "That's the Orthodox way. Are you *that* religious?"

Following a spirited discussion, the committee arrived at a consensus which developed into a conceptual framework. The goal was to create an Adath Jeshurun funeral package which would conform to Jewish tradition. The committee would not become a "consumer" group agitating for lower prices; nor was its goal to lead an attack upon the only Jewish-owned funeral home in the Twin Cities.

The committee agreed to meet monthly to study the Halachic model, the FTC report, and the relevant Minnesota statutes dealing with mortuaries, dead bodies, and related matters. Once this material was sufficiently mastered, the committee would review the "normative" Jewish funeral in our Twin Cities community and the real options available to families.

For several months the committee did its work. As rabbi, I taught the Halacha; an attorney reviewed Minnesota law; a social worker analyzed the FTC report. Members of the committee reacted to these presentations with questions, comments, suggestions, and evaluations.

The study of Halacha convinced the committee that the appropriate model was for the *met* (deceased) to be buried in a simple wood *aron* (coffin). Embalming was not permitted by Jewish law; the *met*, rather, was to be washed ritually in a process called *tahara* (purification) by the Chevra Kadisha (Sacred Society) and then dressed in simple linen *tachrichim* (shrouds).

All of this was rooted in a simple theological concept: dust is to return to dust—as simply and as quickly as possible. In the traditional Jewish model, the Gamaliel principle is operative: in death, everyone is equal. Or, as another sage taught, "There is no dominion on the day of death." What was required was that the *met* be shown *kevod* (honor and respect).

A study of Minnesota law confirmed that, except in rare cases, embalming is not a legal requirement; nor is a vault or grave liner required by state law. It was also quite apparent that the state permits a great deal of leeway to enable people to follow whatever are their religious convictions.

Minnesota law also requires, however, that dead bodies be turned over to a mortuary for "final disposition." Religious groups can follow their traditions, but always under the general aegis of a mortician.

The committee's fifth meeting (in February 1976) was specifically devoted to the issue of the *aron*. It was obvious that a simple wood box was no longer the norm in Jewish funerals. Highly polished and beautifully finished all-wood caskets which were labeled as "Orthodox" hardly conformed to the standards of simplicity. Was the plain pine box not acceptable to the public because of its stark appearance? Or was it a matter of its just not being available in the mortuary inventory?

A personal experience at that time in accompanying a family as it made funeral arrangements confirmed that there was a very cheap (as distinct from inexpensive) all-wood coffin which was not displayed in the selection room. It was available only upon request, and its tawdry, unfinished look discouraged all but the most committed. The price for this box was close to $200, which when added to the other mortuary costs, made the simple funeral not inexpensive.

At the coffee hour that followed the meeting, a committee member familiar with carpentry commented that a simple coffin consists of six pieces of wood: four sides, a top, a bottom. The cost, he insisted, could not be more than $40. Wouldn't it make sense, he wondered, for the congregation to make such a coffin available to every family free of charge? We decided to explore the issue at the following month's meeting.

In March, the committee met—as was its wont—in a private home. A simple wood coffin, fabricated from six pieces of lumber, was brought into the living room. Everyone gasped, for this was the first real object of death to be encountered. Tension was high as the box, which was more than a box, was gingerly inspected. Committee members circled it, and the more hardy touched it.

Then it happened: One of the more daring members offered to get in and try it "for size." Once he lay down in the coffin, it was as if the flood gates had opened. An animated discussion followed.

"Yes, it makes sense to offer a free coffin."

"Why not offer traditional shrouds (*tachrichim*) as well? There are people who are prepared to sew them."

"Should we not assume responsibility for doing the *tahara* (ritual washing of the body)?"

"Could we offer a full traditional funeral free to every member?"

The last question reverberated. Suddenly everyone realized that this was the logical conclusion of the committee's deliberations. Could it be done? And at what cost?

In investigating other funeral models, the committee had learned of the existence of the Minnesota Memorial Society. This group had entered into an arrangement with a cooperating mortuary for a simple funeral at a cost of under $300. Included in this price was a simple coffin, a concrete grave liner, the use of the mortuary chapel for a service, and the professional services of the funeral director.

The Memorial Society model seemed adaptable to our needs. Our own volunteers would provide some of the distinctly Jewish components. If we could contract with a funeral home to transport the *met* from the place of death to the mortuary, where the staff might be generally available to assist our volunteers, perhaps a package could be arranged which would be inexpensive enough to make it possible for Adath Jeshurun to offer a traditional funeral—free—to all its members.

And so it came to pass. The Enga Funeral Home, which cooperated with the Minnesota Memorial Society, offered its services at a price less than half the bid of any other mortuary, including the Jewish-owned funeral home. The decision to abandon the latter was not taken lightly, but the committee felt justified in recommending this action to the congregation's board of directors.

A report was prepared for the congregation board.[2] It recommended, first, that the funeral and burial committee become a standing committee, to be called the Chevra Kevod Hamet—literally, the Society to Honor the Dead. Second, it called upon Adath Jeshurun to provide for all of its members, free of charge, a traditional, or Halachic, funeral package, which would include:

1. A simple wood *aron* which meets Halachic specifications
2. *Tahara* of the *met* to be performed by the congregation's Chevra Kadisha
3. *Tachrichim* sewn by a group of Adath Jeshurun members, so that the *met* may be buried in the time-honored garments used by Jews since the days of Rabbi Gamaliel
4. *Shemira* (watching) of the *met* from the time of death until the actual funeral, to be done by a corps of *shomrim,* so that the *met* not be abandoned.

---

2. See Appendix 1.

In addition, the congregation's contract with Enga called for the latter to transport the *met* from the place of death to the mortuary (where *tahara* would be performed and *shemira* would be done), and from the mortuary to the cemetery. The Chevra would also provide the *shiva* candles and prayer books.

A team of specially trained people called *chaverim* would be assigned to each bereaved family to help in the writing of the obituary, to explain available death benefits (Social Security, veterans, etc.), to contact the cemetery to assure that the grave would be opened, to help, if needed, in the purchase of a plot, and generally to be available as needed during the week of *shiva*. The *chaverim*, in essence, would assume some of the duties generally carried out by funeral directors.

The congregation board also voted to provide seed money to help start the Chevra Kevod Hamet. There was general agreement that voluntary contributions from the bereaved families would be an ongoing source of support for the Chevra's work. The decision by the board of directors to create the Chevra did not automatically assure its success. Many questions remained unanswered:

—Would the Chevra be able to translate its model into action?
—Would members of the congregation trust the Chevra to serve them in time of bereavement?
—Would sufficient volunteers come forward to wash the body, to sit as *shomrim*, to serve as *chaverim*, to sew *tachrichim?*
—Would the congregation accept the decision to utilize Enga rather than the Jewish-owned funeral home?

Today, after well over four years of experience, there is no longer any doubt; the questions have been answered in the affirmative. The Chevra Kevod Hamet has handled close to half the funerals involving Adath Jeshurun members.

There are many volunteers who have agreed to serve in a variety of capacities. The Chevra has captured the popular imagination, and it was the subject of a major TV documentary now available as a 16mm color film.[3] It has been written up in the press, and most recently was cited by Jessica Mitford in her "post-mortem" to the second edition of *The American Way of Death*.[4]

The Chevra's model has also been adapted by Congregation B'nai Torah, Highland Park, Illinois, Congregation Neveh Shalom, Portland, Oregon, and by a consortium of seven congregations in the Washington, D.C., area.

The response of Adath Jeshurun members to the Chevra is a commentary on American Jewish life and the role of the synagogue. The success in attracting volunteers has a significance which transcends the Chevra itself.

---

3. *A Plain Pine Box*, available for purchase through ABC Media and for rental from the National Academy for Adult Jewish Studies, 155 Fifth Avenue, New York, N.Y.

4. Jessica Mitford, *The American Way of Death* (New York: Simon & Schuster, 1978), p. 294.

2

Why Do They Volunteer?

"An Orthodox woman was recently buried in Chicago without a proper *tahara* because the volunteer group of 'dedicated' Orthodox women who are members of the local Chevra Kadisha did not show up in time for the morning *tahara* and the funeral director was unable to secure any other women in time. So much for volunteers."[1]

* * * * * * * *

In *Community and Polity,* his significant work on the institutions of American Jewry, Professor Daniel Elazar writes, "It is safe to say that the American Jewish community boasts the most professional leadership of any in the world, probably the most professional of any in Jewish history. This reflects the commitment to professionalism that is the hallmark of the larger American society."[2]

In contrast to volunteers, professionals who are paid for their services conduct the day-to-day business of all Jewish community institutions, including synagogues. In the latter, rabbis, by virtue of their training, are the logical and accepted spokesmen and leaders. "Rabbis, in fact," Elazar

---

1. Private letter from a mortician in Chicago, October 1, 1976.
2. Daniel Elazar, *Community and Polity* (Philadelphia: Jewish Publication Society, 1976), p. 264.

notes, "are considered successful when they can inspire respect for their professional competence."[3]

The division of the congregation into rabbis and laity has diminished the nonprofessional's role in the synagogue. This, in large measure, is due not only to the training of the rabbis, but also to the low level of Jewish knowledge among non-rabbis. Rabbis in American Jewish life are deferred to because they are the professionals in a society which values professionalism.

The implications of this have been to make the pulpit the center of worship activities, with the service directed by the rabbi and dominated by his personality. "Services," writes Elazar, "have been transformed into orchestrated performances by Americanized Rabbis who . . . assumed ministerial—and later pastoral—functions."[4] "The Protestanization of American life has become the norm."[5] Not only worship, but by extension all synagogue activity, has tended to become a "spectator sport" for most Jews. They listen, they view, they respond on cue; they turn over full responsibility to the functionaries: the rabbi and the cantor—the synagogue "pros."

Sociologist Bernard Reisman, in describing the rise of the *havura,* cites the inevitability of new needs of people not being met by existing institutions. Primary among these needs are community and autonomy.

Synagogues which historically celebrate community, are today not necessarily where Jews turn in order to experience community. Congregations are often viewed primarily as a resource for specific services associated with life's rites of passage, with the initiation and implementation of these rites in the hands of the rabbi and other professionals. Such response as there is tends to be passive and vicarious. Harold

3. Ibid., p. 244.
4. Ibid., p. 90.
5. Ibid., p. 33.

Schulweis, in lamenting this process, has described his typical rabbinic colleague as being "the Jewish cultural and ritual vicar for his congregants. Most members are involved in secondary instrumental activities designed to maintain the institution."[6] Bernard Reisman's critique has been especially sharp: "Temples respond in the same vein as most other modern, impersonal, corporate structures. They have made little significant impact on the alienation of their constituents."[7]

American Jewry is a victim of "surrogatism." Our community has acceded to a process whereby a select few serve as its delegates, deputies, and surrogates. This has intensified a sense of detachment from the synagogue because it does not provide most Jews with a sense of warmth and togetherness. When rabbinical services are needed, they can be purchased "over-the-counter," but, to be sure, for a fee.

Even as rabbi-dominated synagogues often fail to meet the need of community, they have generally failed to perceive the inner yearning many feel for a sense of autonomy. The desire to exercise control over one's own religious life was a primary cause for the creation of the *havura*. Whether or not a *havura* is part of a synagogue, its success is assured only when its members assume responsibility for organizing and conducting services, preparing teaching material, developing a structure, and so forth. In joining others in this enterprise, *havura* members fulfill the twin needs of autonomy and community. The former, flowing from the need to control one's life, is a response to surrogatism; the latter, emanating from the need to resolve tensions and anxieties caused by the craving to be part of something greater than self, is a response to the anomie and alienation felt by modern twentieth-century men and women. The high value placed

---

6. Ibid.
7. Bernard Reisman, "The Havura: An Approach to Humanizing Jewish Organizational Life," *Journal of Jewish Communal Service,* Winter 1975, p. 206.

upon the intimate and autonomous community can be so great that it often overshadows other goals and interests.

Reisman, in describing the success of the *havura,* notes the positives it offers the individual.[8] First and foremost, it is a *primary* experience. Society is centrifugal; the *havura* is centripetal. The *havura* is an opportunity for a meaningful, continuous, personalized, and often intimate, association.

Secondly, it is an autonomous experience. The premise of the *havura* is that people have considerable potential for self-direction; they are far more competent than professionals might be willing to admit. This is an immense appeal in an age when specialization and professionalization have narrowed the realms in which people sense they control their own lives.

Thirdly, the *havura* offers a Jewish outlet; it is precisely the underlying Jewish purpose which is so vital for *havura* participants. They are willing to extend themselves immeasurably to share the Shabbat experience, to celebrate Passover as an extended family, to raise a communal *succah.* Above all, however, there is the drive to study with one another, thereby blurring the distinction between teacher and student. "It is because of the Jewish purpose that the Havurah becomes more than just another transitory social experience."[9]

These three facets of the *havura* experience are replicated in the Chevra. The success of the Chevra Kevod Hamet is related to the willingness of close to two hundred people, of all ages, to assume responsibility for its success. It is not hard to understand why bereaved families turn to the Chevra. For some the Chevra offers a Halachic, or traditionally Jewish, model of burial and grief. For others, it is easier to have the Chevra handle the myriad of details which attend

8. Ibid.

9. Bernard Reisman, *The Havurah: An Evaluative Assessment* (Washington, D.C.: Synagogue Council of America, Analysis no. 63, January 1978), p. 30.

the burial process. For still others, the motivation is economic. It makes sense to save money by turning to the Chevra because a simple funeral will be less expensive. In addition, much of the cost is borne by the congregation. But why do the volunteers agree to serve? What prompts the Chevra Kadisha to handle the *met?* Why do people sit *shemira*—and often at times which are very inconvenient? What motivates busy people to give up time from office or business in order to serve as *chaverim?*

When asked "Why did you become part of the Chevra?" participants offer a variety of responses. The thread in common is the desire to be involved in an authentic Jewish endeavor. Chevra participants perceive themselves as members of a unique community that offers a sense of meaningful association. The Chevra enables them to share with one another a host of experiences growing out of service to their "community." The sense of involvement in this unique enterprise of unusual significance heightens the value of Chevra membership. The "in-group" feeling thus fostered has created—or deepened—friendships.

The Chevra has helped people to become aware of their own competence. With amazement and delight, they learned that they could carry out many of the functions allegedly in the sole domain of the professional funeral director. Chevra members energetically and creatively responded to the challenge to become responsible. It seemed, as if they had been waiting for the opportunity to become so involved. The Chevra attracted people because it was a chance to share in a "hands-on" experience.

Ultimately, however, the Chevra succeeded precisely because people responded to its Jewish dimensions. This underlying Jewishness is vital, for the Chevra is more than a memorial society or a consumer's group. The latter are valid in themselves, but the Chevra meets the deep need felt by many Jews for both a greater understanding of their heritage and an opportunity to translate this heritage into their lives. The Chevra became a challenge to contribute to Jewish continuity, and this endowed their lives with a heightened sense of purpose.

The Chevra, then, may be viewed as a specialized *havura* functioning in the areas of death, grief, and bereavement. Two questions which then follow are: Can the Chevra experience be replicated in other areas of Jewish life? Has Chevra involvement motivated its members to a greater commitment to traditional Jewish life?

Death is obviously a unique area of concern. Interest in the Chevra is undoubtedly due to its challenge to "demystify" death. The Chevra also deals with a built-in socioeconomic issue: the manner in which the funeral director serves the bereaved. Finally, confrontation with death motivates people to consider Jewish tradition, and the Chevra is a challenge to make tradition relevant.

Yet there are other instances where the involvement of "nonprofessionals" could be productive. Some of life's other "passages" also suffer from a neglect of Jewish tradition, from materialistic abuses, from widespread ignorance of how Jews should respond. This has led Harold Schulweis to call for a corps of "pararabbinics" to convey to people a fuller understanding of the Jewish, as well as the emotional, aspects of birth, marriage, conversion. Pararabbinics would help the rabbi, but an enriching experience is assured for those who become part of this group.

The experience of the Chevra Kevod Hamet has demonstrated that the laity can become knowledgeable of the tradition and can then participate in a model in which the skills of the rabbi and the laity, of the professional and the volunteer, are blended.

There are vast areas of Jewish observance, Kashrut, Shabbat, Succot, which can be enriched by rabbinic-lay cooperation. There are many ways in which the interrelated needs of community, autonomy, and Jewishness can be translated into an exciting group process. Synagogues are limited only by their imagination; what is required is the will to act.

While Chevra members are now very comfortable in the congregation and are more often in the synagogue on Shabbat mornings, there have not as yet been great spin-offs of commitment to traditional observances. Chevra members, however, do respond more positively to calls for cooperative activity; for example, they understand how vital it is for every member of the congregation to assume responsibility for the weekday *minyan,* and they support it in greater proportion than other members of the congregation. Chevra members are also more willing to be part of various Torah study groups. Hopefully, as they learn more, they will come to do more.

The Chevra as a Self-Help Group

The Chevra may be defined, sociologically, as a self-help group providing an "episodic" service. Its goal is not only to honor the dead, but also to help the bereaved family re-mobilize its resources. Like many self-help groups, the Chevra is a voluntary group made up of people who feel that a certain need—in this case the needs attendant to handling the dead and strengthening the bereaved—are not being adequately met by or through the existing commerical institutions, and perhaps cannot be.

Self-help groups come in all sizes and shapes, and they provide for a multitude of needs. Generally they fit into one or both of two categories: service, and social advocacy. The former are organized to provide service and/or information; the latter, to change something "out there." The Chevra Kevod Hamet is of the genre which is both service and social advocacy.

Basic to every self-help group is a commitment to autonomy. Self-help groups affirm that, if properly motivated and minimally trained, people will show themselves to be competent.

A basic function of the Chevra is to strengthen the living during bereavement. Like many self-help groups, the Chevra is leery of "professionalism," perceiving it as a process in which responsibility is deflected from the individual to the "expert." The Chevra has succeeded to date because it has keyed into both the desire for autonomy and the sense of urgency felt by so many to be part of something "greater than self." The Chevra, like most self-help groups, challenges "the limitations of a purely pragmatic and bureaucratic society and the impersonal relationship it engenders."[10]

The impersonal quality of the professional mortician's response is precisely the refrain in much of the critical literature on the funeral industry. "The funeral seller, like any other merchant, is preoccupied with price, profit and selling techniques."[11] His casket selection room is logically arranged to stimulate maximum sales; his demeanor of over-solicitous concern is a familiar stereotype.

The Chevra developed because some people felt there had to be a better way to handle funerals. The return to tradition meant a commitment to become personally involved and to join others in working through this involvement. The Chevra sought to restore a personal dimension to caring for the dead and the bereaved. Were it not for the anger felt toward funeral directors and, even more significantly, the sense of frustration engendered by the manner in which Jewish funerals had ceased to reflect Jewish values, the Chevra would never have come into being. Self-help groups posit that

---

10. Kurt Back and Rebecca Taylor, "Self-Help Groups: Tool or Symbol?" *Journal of Applied Behavior Science* 12, no. 3 (July 1976):305.

11. Jessica Mitford, *The American Way of Death* (New York: Simon & Schuster, 1978), p. 23.

professionals are not omnipotent; members of the Chevra share this view regarding funeral directors and even rabbis. The inability of critics of the Chevra to understand this explains why time and again focus is directed on the "economic" implications of the Chevra.

Back and Taylor observe that "modernization and social development are, in great part, increasing divisions of labor and professionalization of work with an increased appeal to reason, knowledge and technology to solve the problems that occur during human life."[12] As more and more people become increasingly uncomfortable with science and technology as sources which can invest their lives with meaning, there has been a corresponding response to reduce life to its basics. This has led some to communes, where personal labor is exalted and where individuals forge for themselves life's essentials. A more moderate response has been to explore ways in which an individual can remain within society's mainstream and yet serve himself and others. These efforts, while lacking the crispness and the sharpness of the specialist or expert, build upon the individual's talents and abilities. The Chevra, then, is appropriately perceived as a reaction to the smooth efficiency which characterizes the funeral professional.

Yet even self-help groups must be sensitive to the tendency to become overly structured and bureaucratized. Katz and Bender have charted the process of a group's growth and change: (1) the original charismatic leadership is replaced; (2) a bureaucratic structure emerges; (3) a general accommodation to society occurs; and (4) participants develop an interest in the group's maintenance, regardless of the group's ability to maintain its goals.[13]

---

12. Back and Taylor, "Self-Help Groups," p. 302.

13. Alfred Katz and Eugene Bender, *The Strength in Us: Self-Help Groups in the Modern World* (New York: Franklin Watts, 1976), p. 281.

Katz has applied this model to self-help groups, noting a "natural history of five stages typical of their growth: (1) origin; (2) informal organizational phase; (3) emergence of leadership; (4) beginnings of formal organization; and (5) paid staff workers and professionals."[14]

The Chevra has worked through the first four steps of Katz's model. It enjoys good leadership and it is formally organized. Should there be an attrition of concerned leadership or should the volunteerism which has characterized it to date fail to perpetuate itself, the Chevra will have one of two options. It can turn to professional help, whether this be existing congregational staff or specifically employed personnel, or it can disband.

The Chevra's success in recruiting members will depend upon three factors: the support given the Chevra by the congregation, the effectiveness of the Chevra's leadership in maintaining a high profile within the congregation, and the ability of the Chevra to sensitize the congregation members to a Halachic value system which insists that people assume personal responsibility to care for the dead and strengthen the living.

Success in the last-named area will assure success in all three areas. A solid educational program has helped assure continued support of the Chevra by congregational leaders. Education and sensitization, important goals of the Chevra, are assigned to two committees, one concerned with education, the other with medical ethics.[15] The education committee which assumes responsibility for reaching the membership, schedules special programs, open to the entire congregation, wherein the Chevra story is told and retold. These programs include such activities as showing relevant films, inviting knowledgeable speakers, and organizing special Shabbat Eve

14. Ibid.
15. See below Chapter 6.

pulpit presentations. The education committee is also charged with publishing material on the Chevra in the congregational bulletin. One of its goals is to publish a manual describing a traditional funeral and how the Chevra specifically functions in this context. This manual being prepared by a subcommittee on which the rabbi serves as a member and as a resource person will reflect rabbinic-lay interaction.

As more people learn of the work of the Chevra, the number of volunteers asking to share in its work increases.

*   *   *   *   *   *   *   *

One member of the Chevra stated her reason for joining the Chevra: "I wanted to perform a service to those in need which, in turn, would strengthen our tradition. Every time I'm called upon to perform a service, I feel an inner sense of gratification and a strengthening of a bond between me and the congregation."

3

Acceptance and Resistance

> No one thought we'd ever get off
> the ground. After all, this is
> America—the great death-denial
> society.
>
> —DR. ALAN BRISKIN

The willingness of many Adath Jeshurun members to be served by the Chevra does not mean that the entire congregational membership of eleven hundred families is committed to the program. The majority of members have not completed the "Expression of Guidance,"[1] and a minority have reacted negatively to the Chevra concept. The latter's objections generally flow from a misunderstanding of what comprises a traditional Jewish funeral, a perception that a person's standard of living should be reflected at his death, and difficulty in dealing with the inevitability—and finality—of death.

The Traditional Funeral: A Model

The mandates of Halacha have ceased to be a force in the lives of most American Jews. As American Jewry acculturates, it takes on more and more of the values and practices of the dominant Christian society. Both sociologists and

---

1. See Appendix 2.

rabbis have documented the erosion of traditional Jewish values, which has had a wide-ranging effect on all areas of individual and communal life, including funeral practices.

For many Jews, a "traditional" Jewish funeral is one modeled on the American: expensive caskets (even if wood); massive concrete vaults, complete with personalized covers which, when set into place, seal themselves automatically and hermetically; embalmed bodies; burial in suits or dresses rather than *tachrichim;* draping of the casket with an imitation grass carpet during the interment service; and the departure of the family and friends from the grave site prior to burial. Two generations of such practices have created a new American Jewish tradition. Given the human propensity to like what you know rather than to know what you like, it is natural for many Jews to reject as "untraditional" a traditional funeral model that has become foreign to them. Memory seldom reaches back to the past's prevailing custom. Our investment in the way we do things makes it difficult to contemplate any changes.

The Halachic model, with its call for simplicity, direct participation in the burial, *tachrichim,* and so on, is viewed by many modern-day Jews as medieval at best, and barbaric at worst. To some, it is a reversion to a pattern better left in the past; to others, its departure from the status quo makes it automatically suspect.

The Jewish public cannot really be held responsible for accepting the contemporary Jewish funeral as being authentically Jewish, since the rabbinate, for a variety of reasons, has not challenged the abandonment of the Halachic model. Rabbis have allowed the Jewish funeral industry to serve the community without any sustained challenge. True, individual rabbis have demanded that certain standards be met; in some communities certain practices considered too Gentile have been challenged and changed, the most common being the visitation at the chapel the night before the funeral, even if the casket be closed. It is interesting that once the voice of a united rabbinate was raised in protest, this practice—an obvious imitation of Gentile tradition—was ended. Visitation remains, to date, the one issue in which Jewish funeral directors have had to accede to rabbinic sentiment and control. The Jewish public, as it came to understand that visitation was not the Jewish way, followed rabbinic direction. With no united rabbinic voice protesting other practices, the public can hardly be blamed for assuming that what is available at the Jewish funeral home is appropriately, and even authentically, Jewish. One observer states it simply: "Most Jews, in fact, assume that at a Jewish funeral home, they are obtaining a Jewish funeral."

Standards of Living in Death

Kramer and Leventman, in their classic sociological study of the Jewish community of Minneapolis, *Children of the Gilded Ghetto,* describe two funerals. Mr. Philip Robbins, a wealthy merchant, was buried in a "fashionable walnut casket." Mr. Joseph Goldberg, a retired tailor, was interred in a "plain pine box." The authors quote the Jewish funeral director, who defended the differences. "Goldberg was buried in a 'plain pine box' by a family which believes in putting people into the ground as *cheaply* as possible. A family spends in death as they do in life. If a person drove a Cadillac, chances are that the funeral will show it and will differ from that of a person who drove a Ford."[2]

There is no doubt that many people believe it inappropriate to alter an economic life-style when it comes to a casket purchase. They reject the tradition's demand for simplicity because they reject the tradition's rationale that in death, all are equal.

---

2. J. R. Kramer and S. Leventman, *Children of the Gilded Ghetto* (New Haven: Yale Univ. Press, 1961), p. 60.

Often families which might prefer to opt for less ostentatious, and hence less expensive, funerals are concerned lest they appear "cheap" in the eyes of friends and community. Since the Halachic model is not understood, the tendency is to conform to prevailing patterns.

In a private discussion, a leading Jewish funeral director insisted that the "original" Jewish tradition allowed funerals in line with a family's purse. Gamaliel's ruling was a departure from the way Jews traditionally handled their dead, and, in our day, American Jewry has simply returned to the true tradition of funerals according to one's means.

To those Jews who are committed to the more expensive, to the "top of the line," the Chevra and its Halachic guidelines based on simplicity cannot be acceptable.

Denial of Death

Dr. Herman Feifel, a leading psychologist, has observed that death may be viewed as either a doorway or a wall.[3] When the religious view predominated, people regarded death as a door leading to a better and truer existence in a beautiful otherworld which mortals could never truly comprehend.

A Jew, for example, who accepted the rabbinic view set down in the *Ethics of the Fathers* that "This world is but a corridor leading to the world-to-come" could find great support when confronted with death. To the bereaved, it meant that his or her beloved was now in the true world; to the person in death throes, there was the comfort that death was the final door through which we pass prior to our final judgment and reward!

In our sophisticated age, values have changed. With belief in afterlife fading, more and more people now perceive death as a wall. Death is regarded as the end point where the trip through life terminates.

---

3. Herman Feifel, *New Meanings of Death* (New York: McGraw-Hill, 1977).

"Death is seen as the destroyer of the American vision—the right to life, liberty and the pursuit of happiness. Hence death and dying invite our hostility and repudiation."[4] Our own experience corroborates the tendency of disguising death and pretending that it is not a condition of life.

Geoffrey Gorer, an English psychologist, insists that in this century, death has become the new pornography; it is the subject polite society has banned from social discourse. Despite the spate of books on death published during the past decade, and despite death having become a respectable field of inquiry in the social and behavioral sciences, most Americans continue to deny the reality and the inevitablity of death.

Few people seem emotionally capable of grappling with the penetrating insight that except statistically, dying is not an eventuality of old age; it is an eventuality of each moment. We are terrified of death, and we handle our fear by seeking to repress the fact that death is the common fate of all who live.

The process of death-denial has gone hand in hand with the transfer of the "dying process" from home to hospital. Death comes stealthily, as it were, to hidden corners of our society: the hospitals and the special wards for the dying. When death does occur, the dead are removed from sight in a judicious and efficient transfer from hospital to funeral home.

At one time Jews, like many other peoples, involved themselves in the actual handling of the dead, in "laying out" the deceased and preparing him or her for burial. Today, this task has been relegated to the mortician, and in the process, death has all but disappeared from our view. Our lapse into death-denial is reinforced by the notion that what you don't see doesn't exist.

---

4. Ibid., p. 5.

The funeral industry is sensitive to the American distaste for confrontation with death. This mood is reflected in the industry's terminology. People don't die, they "pass on." Embalming is designed to make the corpse "lifelike." The casket, complete with mattress (often innerspring, no less), is to assure maximum "comfort." The actual interment is not carried out in public view, much less is it an act in which family and friends may participate. The cemetery has become a memorial park. The undertaker is a grief counselor. Death has seemingly disappeared from our midst. Seemingly, but not really.

The Chevra, with its message of pre-need arrangements, challenges this denial syndrome. The Halachic model, which demands actual involvement with the body, whether it be through participation in the Chevra Kadisha or through sitting *shemira,* does not permit the luxury of denying death. The insistence that the final kindness we can perform for the dead is to share in his or her burial by helping fill in the grave rejects the prevailing view that we should not confront death.

While many people take out life insurance and write wills, few people make pre-need arrangements with cemeteries and mortuaries; it is threatening to prepare for your own funeral and burial. This accounts for the relatively few "Expressions of Guidance" filed with our congregation. Even where the Chevra has served a family, there was often no signed "Expression of Guidance." Only after the death did the family turn to the Chevra.

The Chevra continues to sensitize people to the reality of death. Its education committee has developed materials which, together with pulpit presentations, have enabled it to heighten awareness and sensitivity. More and more people have come to respond to the Chevra's motto: "To honor the dead; to strengthen the living." Progress, of course, is often imperceptible. There seems to be a growing sensitivity that death comes not to the dead, but to the living, and that we, the living, must prepare ourselves for it. Whether we will it or not, death is real; for most of us, bereavement is inevitable. How we prepare ourselves for death grows out of our philosophy of life and death. Given Judaism's commitment to equality, plus the belief that "there is no dominion on the day of death," Jews should bury simply and quickly, with every *met* treated alike.

Death, in Judaism, is more than a biological occurrence; it is a social experience involving our response as a community.

4

The Memorial Society:

An Alternative Model

Memorial societies were founded in 1939. They are consumer "co-ops" organized on a not-for-profit basis for the single purpose of providing information and assistance regarding low-cost funeral arrangements. Unlike most co-ops, however, memorial societies do not directly provide their members with any services or goods. The society, instead, enters into a contract with a cooperating mortuary which assumes responsibility for handling the dead. The memorial society, in actuality, does not compete with any funeral home.

The society's overall goal is to promote simple, dignified, and economical funerals through advance or pre-need planning. Memorial societies discourage ostentatious caskets, costly extras, unnecessary embalming, public display and viewing of the body, and elaborate floral displays. In lieu of flowers, contributions to "living programs," usually funds for medical research, are encouraged.

The funeral industry has consistently deprecated memorial societies as being concerned merely with the disposal of the body but not with any rituals surrounding burial. This, to some extent, is true; but it is the societies' focus on simplicity and price, with its negative effect upon profit margins which distresses the funeral industry. The emphasis on pre-need planning is also a threat to the industry, since a family dealing with a mortuary during the brief period between death and burial has virtually no bargaining power. The family members in that instance are captives, especially since they are often traumatized. As consumers, they are vulnerable.

A rabbinic interpretation of the verse in Leviticus, "Do not place a stumbling-block before the blind," broadened the text to protect more than the sightless. The rabbis taught that a person who is vulnerable or ignorant must be protected from abuse. Judaism never accepted caveat emptor—"let the buyer beware"—as a morally valid commercial principle. Many centuries later, the U.S. Supreme Court, in the *Keppel* case, substantiated concern for the vulnerable consumer. "Because of imbalance in the bargaining power, sellers abuse their superior position and consumers are unable to protect themselves."[1]

A congregational policy, then, encouraging pre-need arrangements in which a standard package of basic services—the type of coffin and the cost structure—was established in advance, seemed Halachically responsible. A study of Halachic literature, in fact, may even require such congregational intervention. The Halacha forbids windfall profits and taking advantage of the uninformed or helpless buyer (or seller). Where such inequities occur, the Halacha does not permit us to sit by silently and unconcerned, because neutrality in such situations does not help the disadvantaged.

Early in the Chevra's development, a meeting was arranged with the director of the Minnesota Memorial Society (MMS), to learn more about its model. Membership, acquired through a one-time payment of a modest fee, is transferable, should a family relocate, to the memorial soci-

---

1. *FTC v. Keppel*, 29 U.S. 304.

ety in another area. An umbrella organization, the Continental Association of Memorial Societies, keeps state societies in contact with one another. During the past decade, a momentum has developed and memorial society memberships have increased manyfold. The discussion also brought to light that few Jews were members of the Minnesota Memorial Society and that no congregation had developed a program to qualify for membership in the Continental Association.

Locally, the MMS had arranged with several mortuaries to provide a simple funeral which included a plain wood coffin, a concrete grave liner, the funeral chapel for a service (if requested), the use of the hearse to transport the body to the cemetery or crematorium, and the overall services of the mortuary personnel. The cost, then, was $275.

The study committee's first reaction was that such a model, properly adapted, would be acceptable Halachically. The established cost of $275 was low enough so that the congregation, seeking to stimulate Halachic funerals, could provide the same, free of charge, to all of its members.

There were, of course, some basic differences between the memorial society model and what the study committee saw itself as trying to accomplish. The memorial society, concerned primarily with economic abuses, is essentially a broker bringing together family and mortician. From that point on, the latter assumes responsibility for preparing the deceased for burial. The Chevra model demanded direct committee involvement in various facets of the process. It was vital that the Chevra Kadisha perform the *tahara* and that *shomrim* watch the body until the funeral. It was also essential that representatives of the Chevra, called *chaverim,* be available to the family to aid in the arrangements. All in all, the Chevra had the volunteers; what was needed was a cooperating mortuary which would allow the use of its facilities for the ritual preparations.

The mortuary's expertise might also be needed to help write an occasional obituary, to arrange for local burial in the event of an out-of-state death, to negotiate with a cemetery to open a grave. The mortuary was also to transport the deceased from the place of death to the chapel, and from there to the cemetery—with a possible intermediary stop at the synagogue, should the service be held there.

Letters were sent by the Chevra to the mortuaries which cooperated with the Minnesota Memorial Society, indicating our needs and inviting these firms to bid on the "package." The most competitive bid was from the Enga Funeral Home, and it was invited to serve the Chevra and Adath Jeshurun. Enga already had experience with various ethnic groups which involved their members in the handling of their dead. Enga was thus easily sensitized to the specifically Jewish needs of the Chevra. Enga's price for its services and facilities was under $300, with the congregation providing the coffin. Enga also agreed to set aside a cabinet where the Chevra might store the pails, aprons, boots, and other paraphernalia needed by the Chevra Kadisha. There would also be a bookcase for the books and pamphlets needed for the *shomrim*.

Enga, however, was not the Jewish-owned mortuary in the community. Experience had shown that "most Jews, observant or not, will patronize Jewish funeral homes when they are available."[2] The Chevra had no intention of engaging in a vendetta against the local Jewish-owned mortuary. There was for the Chevra a two-part goal: to restore Halacha as a viable option for those who desired it, and to establish a process whereby Adath Jeshurun members might involve themselves in performing the *mitzva* of *kevod hamet*. The Chevra also desired that the synagogue provide the funeral as a privilege of membership.

---

2. *Toward New Policies on Jewish Funeral Practices* (Washington, D.C.: Institute for Jewish Policy Planning and Research, Synagogue Council of America, Analysis no. 56, April 1976), p. 4.

Before negotiating with Enga, a meeting was arranged between some of the Chevra leaders and the heads of the local Jewish-owned mortuary. This firm, which had served Twin Cities Jewry for many decades, perceived itself, and was perceived by many, as a community institution. Early in the meeting, it became apparent that the Chevra and the funeral directors had different views of what Halacha demanded. The latter were skeptical about "volunteers" doing *tahara* or *shemira,* and saw little need for *chaverim.* In general, the Chevra's goal of involving people was not seen in a positive light. Having served the Jewish community for these many years, the president of the firm regarded himself as more of an authority on the components of a Jewish funeral than the synagogue's rabbi.

When the discussion moved to cost, the Chevra learned that the funeral home insisted upon maintaining its basic cost for professional services and facility use, without any reduction to the congregation. A subsequent private visit with the funeral home officers by a member of the Chevra was unsuccessful in effecting any change in cost structure.

The Chevra was now confronted with a serious question: should it stay with the Jewish-owned funeral home, or enter into a relationship with a Gentile-owned firm? After careful consideration, the Chevra recommended that Enga be the cooperating mortuary.[3] There was an awareness within the Chevra that this decision would spark some community controversy. No one really foresaw how intense it would be.

Unknown to the Chevra as it engaged in its deliberations, a task force of the Synagogue Council of America was preparing its own study of Jewish funeral practices. These

---

3. A contributing factor to the decision was that many of the professional personnel of the Jewish-owned home were not Jewish. Since the development of the Chevra Kevod Hamet, that firm has adopted a policy of hiring only Jewish funeral directors. The final irony is that a non-Jewish funeral director, who had been on the Jewish-owned home's staff for over a decade and had arranged hundreds of Jewish funerals, is now on the staff of Enga.

findings were published almost on the very date when the Chevra submitted its final report to the board. Many of the Chevra's findings and recommendations paralleled those of the Synagogue Council. Of special interest was the latter's discussion of memorial societies and their applicability to the Jewish community. The Synagogue Council encouraged Jews to form such societies in order to deal with Jewish-owned funeral homes, but "if local funeral establishments under Jewish ownership are unwilling to cooperate with such memorial societies, a Jewish group could also consider turning to nonsectarian funeral homes. Such cooperating homes would contract to comply with Jewish requirements and be overseen in this regard by members of the Chevra Kadisha."[4]

A significant factor in the decision to use Enga was that a Jewish-owned funeral home is, in fact, a private business with an appropriate and understandable interest in profit. It is not a community institution, automatically providing a "Jewish" funeral conforming to Halachic standards. The Synagogue Council's report noted that even where the operators of a Jewish funeral home are aware of Jewish traditions regarding death, burial, and grief, "the commercialization of these sacred functions (even if there are no exploitive abuses), distorts traditional Jewish values."[5]

Concern with tradition motivated the Chevra. There was always a temptation to deal with economic issues, but the Chevra never followed the memorial society's lead in challenging the funeral industry's price structure. The Chevra's goal was to develop a process which would sensitize Adath Jeshurun members to Halachic requirements while creating conditions in which people would be comfortable opting for the Halachic model.

---

4. *Toward New Policies on Jewish Funeral Practices*, p. 4.
5. Ibid., p. 5.

5

Responses and Reactions

Rabbinic

The May 1976 decision of the Adath Jeshurun board of directors to accept the recommendation to offer a free traditional funeral was featured in a front-page story in the *Clarion,* the congregation's weekly bulletin. The Chevra model was also discussed from the pulpit on the second day of the festival of Shavuot (Pentecost) in the context of the special holiday *Yizkor* (memorial) service.

During the beautiful but all too brief summer, Minnesotans generally declare a moratorium on committee activity. There was thus very little reaction to the Chevra; in fact, it seemed to be dormant. In actuality, however, Chevra leaders were making plans to become operational with the start of the new Jewish year of 5737 (October 1976).

The Chevra Kadisha met to develop its procedures; the *chaverim* planned an in-service training session; the *shomrim* committee organized its procedures; the first *aronot* (coffins) were being built; *tachrichim* were sewn; and Enga and the Chevra leadership were in constant contact.

In August 1976, the entire synagogue membership was again informed by letter of the existence of the Chevra. Included in the mailing was the "Expression of Guidance" in which people could specify their desire to have their funerals taken care of by the Chevra.[1] The congregation assumed the responsibility of sending copies of completed "Expressions" to parties designated by the enrollee (attorneys, next of kin, etc.).

The fall editions of the *Clarion* included material on the Chevra, thereby heightening sensitivity to—and awareness of—the program. During this time, the overall Jewish community took little notice of the Chevra. Many viewed it as another gambit on the part of a rabbi for publicity or notoriety. Others warned that it was a foolish project, doomed to failure because the volunteers, despite their good intentions, would never really be available to serve bereaved families, and especially to handle dead bodies. Some people agreed that the Chevra raised valid questions about Jewish funerals in the Twin Cities, but since there was no burning desire for change, this reform, too, would peter out.

The Jewish-owned funeral home was concerned, but not overly so. Virtually all prior rabbinic attempts to reform funeral practices had failed, and there was little reason to believe that this latest effort would succeed. Yet, following the adage that an ounce of prevention is better than a pound of cure, the president of the Jewish-owned mortuary contacted the president of the Minnesota Rabbinical Association (MRA) to solicit an invitation to appear before the rabbis. The purpose was to discuss areas of mutual concern. This meeting was set for late October, after the fall holiday season.

Twin Cities rabbinic responses to the Chevra ranged from negative to cynical. One rabbi, in his first reaction, spoke for many when he contended that the congregation was sure to lose because "no one would go for it." The rabbinic consensus was that while some changes would be beneficial, the massive changes advocated by Adath Jeshurun, relying so

---

1. See Appendix 2.

heavily on volunteers, could never be carried off. In addition, there was overt rabbinic dissatisfaction that Enga would be used rather than the Jewish-owned home. Since no one outside Adath Jeshurun really expected the Chevra to succeed, the issue was not addressed, during the summer of 1976, by the Minnesota rabbinate.

My sermon at the Adath Jeshurun Congregation on the first day of Rosh Hashana was devoted, in part, to the Chevra Kevod Hamet and its formal beginnings. It was a spirited pulpit defense of the Chevra model, and congregation members were urged to view with pride this attempt to make Halacha viable. A summary of the sermon and a press release announcing that the Chevra was operational were sent to the two Minneapolis papers: the *Morning Tribune* and the *Afternoon Star*. Both papers considered the Chevra story important. On Saturday morning, October 1, 1976, the first day of Rosh Hashana, the *Minneapolis Tribune* published a front-page story on the Chevra, complete with interviews with some of the Chevra leadership.

The local AP stringer in Minneapolis put the story on the wires, and on Sunday, October 2, the birth of the Chevra was announced in papers throughout the country, including the *New York Times*. From that time on, the Chevra ceased being but a local story; it was now watched in many other communities as a congregational effort to change the accepted community pattern of funeral practices.

This publicity triggered a response within the Twin Cities Jewish community. Rabbi Marc Liebhaber, in his column in the weekly *American Jewish World,* attacked Adath Jeshurun and its rabbi, accusing them of conducting a vendetta against the Jewish-owned funeral home in the community.[2] To Rabbi Liebhaber, there were two issues: the propriety of an individual rabbi taking any action in an attempt to change

2. *American Jewish World* (Minneapolis), October 15, 1976, p. 2.

a community pattern, and the audacity of the congregation in inviting a nonsectarian funeral home to handle Jewish funerals. From the tone and content of the article, it was apparent that Rabbi Liebhaber did not understand the concept of the Chevra. Yet he did raise what was to become a front-burner issue: the choice of Enga over the Jewish-owned funeral home.

The Chevra's position was articulated very clearly in several responses which appeared in the following issue of the *American Jewish World*.[3] Rabbi Liebhaber's allegation of a vendetta against the Jewish-owned home was vigorously denied. The responses contended that the Chevra did not have as its target any single funeral chapel.

> Neither the Chevra nor anyone speaking on behalf of the Adath Jeshurun had suggested that a funeral home was anything more than a private enterprise with the right to determine its own business policies, prices, etc. It was on the basis of free enterprise that, after careful consideration and responsible negotiation, the Chevra Kevod Hamet made its decision on which funeral home was most suited for its purposes.[4]

Rabbi Liebhaber's accusation that the entire project was little more than an extension of the rabbinic arm brought forth a forceful statement by the Adath Jeshurun leadership that the Chevra had been created by a board decision after deliberate discussion and debate.

The issue was now joined, and the Jewish community found itself embroiled in controversy. Was the Chevra really needed, since people could always arrange for a traditional funeral in the Jewish-owned home? If Adath Jeshurun wanted to develop its own volunteer program, should it have

---

3. Ibid., October 22, 1976, pp. 1, 3, 4.
4. Ibid., p. 1.

turned to Enga? For some, Enga was a poor choice because Jews should support Jews; others, in turn, were concerned about utilizing a Gentile home for Jewish funerals. There were some who agreed with Rabbi Liebhaber that the Chevra was a personal attack by an individual rabbi on the Jewish-owned funeral home. Others wondered why this was a "solo" project of one congregation, for if the criticisms raised by the Chevra were valid, why were the other rabbis (and congregations) at best silent, and at worst, openly opposed? There was also criticism of what was perceived to be the entry of Adath Jeshurun into the funeral business. Little wonder that the Chevra—its virtues and its shortcomings—became a subject of heated debate as proponents and opponents reacted to this congregational program.

For a month and a half, the issue remained academic; the Chevra had not handled any funerals. Then, on Tuesday evening, November 4, 1976, the first call came in and the Chevra was faced with its first test. Within twenty-four hours it was apparent that the volunteers had successfully interfaced with the Enga staff and the rabbi. The *met* was washed, dressed in *tachrichim,* and placed in the Chevra's specially designed coffin. The *shomrim* were there throughout the entire night and morning, and the *chaverim* provided great support for the bereaved. The family was satisfied with the entire process.

The obituary notice placed in the paper reported "Arrangements by the Enga Funeral Home and the Adath Jeshurun Chevra Kevod Hamet." This first Chevra involvement in serving a family vested the issue with new significance. The Chevra had moved from theory to action and from the abstract to the concrete!

The MRA now began an earnest discussion of the issues, not the least of which was whether a congregation had the right to take unilateral action in an area of such great interest to every rabbi. Many MRA members contended that the association had taken some limited stands on funeral practices—primarily the unanimous rabbinic decision opposing viewing of the body, visitation the night before the funeral and open caskets at the service. This edict, supported by the Jewish-owned funeral home, had become the accepted practice in the Twin Cities Jewish community.

The MRA had also issued a statement setting down guidelines for funeral practices.[5] Since community rabbinic associations, which comprise rabbis of all denominations, agree not to take stands on Halachic issues, the MRA guidelines, therefore, were general and often vague. The call for an end to ostentation, for example, lent itself to different interpretations. My contention was that the action of Adath Jeshurun did not contravene any MRA policy; on the contrary, it was consistent with the spirit of the existing guidelines.

The MRA consensus was that the right of Adath Jeshurun to establish its Chevra could not be challenged. MRA members objected to the implication that only the Chevra Kevod Hamet provided traditional and dignified funerals, in contrast to practices in other congregations and by other rabbis. While Adath Jeshurun had neither said nor even implied this, a very scrutinized in-between-lines study of the press stories could lend this impression. Rabbis, who are trained to read for comprehension on many levels, very naturally concluded that they were being treated unfairly by the press and by Adath Jeshurun.

The most highly charged issue before the MRA, however, concerned the "abandonment" of the Jewish-owned funeral home and the impact of this decision upon the community. The previous spring's almost casual request by the president of the Jewish-owned mortuary to appear before the rabbis

---

5. See Appendix 3.

was now elevated into an urgent demand. Pressure was exerted upon the MRA membership to pass a resolution which would support—and praise—the Jewish-owned funeral home, its manner of service to the Jewish community, and the "Jewishness" of that service. The MRA was also encouraged to include in this resolution an explicit, or, at the very least, an implicit, criticism of the Adath Jeshurun Congregation and its Chevra Kevod Hamet.

The session with the heads of the Jewish-owned home took place at the MRA meeting on November 6, 1976. The Jewish-owned home was represented by its president and vice-president, plus the legal counsel and president of the Jewish Funeral Directors Association (JFDA). The Jewish-owned home's representatives distributed a well-prepared "book" which contained, among other documents, the exchange of letters between the mortuary's president and the chairperson of the then study committee of Adath Jeshurun, a summary financial statement justifying the funeral home's cost structure, and a detailed refutation of allegations made from the Adath Jeshurun pulpit concerning Jewish funeral practices, whether in sermons or in published materials.

At the December meeting of the MRA, Dr. Alan Briskin, the Chevra Kevod Hamet chairperson, appeared; he reiterated the positions as I had defined them.

In January of 1977, a group of rabbis, all but one of whom were members of the MRA, but excluding me, met privately. At that time they agreed upon a resolution which was openly supportive and laudatory of the Jewish funeral home and explicitly critical of the Adath Jeshurun Congregation. This resolution, circulated among MRA members, was placed on the agenda of the next MRA meeting.

The debate that followed indicated the need for a special meeting to resolve the issue. A three-man subcommittee was formed to develop a new resolution which would be acceptable to the entire MRA. Since I was one of the three subcommittee members, there was hope that this goal might be achieved. Unfortunately, no agreement was reached, and the subcommittee majority prepared its own resolution.

An all-morning special MRA meeting took place on March 21, 1977. The majority resolution was placed before the MRA. After much discussion a resolution was passed.[6] While substantially toned down from January's "private" resolution, it was still very supportive of the manner in which Jewish funerals were being handled within the community. It did, however, affirm the legitimacy of all views of *kevod hamet.* After much deliberation, the resolution passed with my abstention. Since the reputation of Adath Jeshurun was involved, I indicated a desire to discuss my vote with the congregational leaders. The MRA membership viewed this as an appropriate response; it was agreed not to publicize the resolution for two weeks. During that time, the Adath Jeshurun leadership would have ample time to discuss my abstention and decide whether it should be changed to a yea. Ten days later I informed the MRA secretary that I would vote in favor of the resolution. This made it unanimous.

Before the resolution could be published, the president of the Jewish-owned funeral home died. His funeral was attended by over a thousand people. Five rabbis, spanning the gamut from Orthodox to Reform, eulogized him. Each extolled his role within the community. The final eulogy was delivered by the deceased's rabbi, an outspoken opponent of the Chevra. He wove into his eulogy an attack, albeit implicitly, on the Chevra Kevod Hamet and the Adath Jeshurun pulpit. Although the deceased's heart condition was well known, the eulogy all but laid the blame for his death upon the proponents of the Chevra Kevod Hamet. For many rabbis, this public attack placed the confrontation in a new light. Since the controversy, in large part, revolved around

---

6. See Appendix 4.

the deceased's intense feelings as well as the personal affection for him, his death made much of the debate moot. The MRA, in essence, closed out the issue by passing a mild resolution with which everyone could agree.[7]

The Chevra, however, was reinforced by the decision of ABC to make it the subject of an "on-site" documentary for national TV as part of the *Directions* series. The program, first shown on October 23, 1977, and preceded by ample publicity, heightened public awareness. It also intensified a process which had predictably begun to unfold in the relatively small Twin Cities Jewish community. Practices or programs adopted in one congregation have an effect and an impact upon other congregations. As members of other congregations made *shiva* (condolence) calls to—or were relatives of—bereaved families served by the Chevra, pressures were felt by other rabbis to respond to the issues raised by the Chevra. While no Twin Cities congregation has, to date, adopted the Adath Jeshurun model, several synagogues do have funeral-practices committees which are exploring models to enable their members to be more effectively supported during bereavement.

Whatever else may be said about the Chevra, it is obvious that families now have an option or an alternative in deciding upon funeral arrangements. The Chevra has not destroyed the Jewish-owned funeral home, nor has it embarrassed other rabbis. It has helped make Halachic burials more of a norm.

It is of more than passing interest that as an increasing number of Twin Cities Jewish families opted for wood coffins, the Jewish-owned funeral home raised the price of lower-end funerals. The decision of more people to choose

---

7. The resolution affirmed that the deceased had worked closely with the rabbinical community in maintaining care and respect for the dead and mourners in our community.

less expensive funerals made it necessary to raise prices in order to sustain the firm's profit margin.

This is a tacit admission that the Jewish-owned funeral home is a private enterprise before all else.

The Community

The community response was varied. The major criticisms were from long-time friends and associates of the president of the Jewish-owned funeral home and his family. Since many of the people involved in the Chevra were "newcomers" to Minneapolis (i.e., they were not born in the Twin Cities), it was not surprising that the Chevra was viewed as an attack by strangers on a community institution.

For years the Jewish community had responded to death by notifying the one Jewish-owned mortuary. Not many people seemed to notice or care that while the heads of the firm were Jewish, their employees, including other directors who helped arrange funerals, were not. The Jewish-owned funeral home managed to project the image of being a Jewish communal institution. No one disputed its Jewishness despite the fact that the major contact of a grieving family was often with a non-Jew. Few challenged its communal status although the firm was, and still is, a private business interested in making a profit. Its status in the Jewish community was so widely accepted that the Adath Jeshurun Congregation was accused of trying to rupture the community by destroying one of its major institutions.

Preserving community unity is a primary agenda item of the Minneapolis Federation for Jewish Services. As the centralized fund-raiser for Israel and most domestic Jewish causes, Federation is perceived in Minneapolis, as elsewhere, as the primary institution within the Jewish community. Federations have involved themselves in community planning and tend to consider themselves the arbiters of all that is beneficial to the Jewish community.

Daniel Elazar has graphically described the growth of Federations during the last two decades. "After 1960, Federations increasingly began to define the range of their interests as embracing virtually the total Jewish community, excluding only the synagogues."[8] "Each congregation," Elazar continues, "is independent in every respect, a Jewish world unto itself, so to speak, at least insofar as it wants to be."[9] Again, "the synagogues remain the most independent institutions in the American Jewish community, fiscally self-sufficient, subject to no communal discipline (except in the subtle ways that influence all Jews). American synagogues have traditionally considered themselves (and have been considered) private institutions . . . accountable to no one but their own members."[10]

Minneapolis generally parallels the national process. The local Federation continues to expand its hegemony, with the synagogues remaining independent. There is, to be sure, active cooperation between congregations and Federation, and given a community synagogue affiliation rate of 75–80 percent, no Federation leader has ever been "unsynagogued." Yet, while all pulpit rabbis are invited to serve on the Federation board, no rabbi is on the executive committee, where most decisions are made. In addition, whenever there is a conflict between Federation and a synagogue, it is the latter that is expected to give way. The rationale is almost a litany: "The community comes first; community unity must be maintained—at whatever the cost!"

The controversy which erupted within the community due to Adath Jeshurun's decision to utilize the services of a non-Jewish funeral home disturbed Federation's leaders. The family proprietors of the Jewish-owned mortuary were—and are—contributors to Federation, and they de-

---

8. Daniel Elazar, *Community and Polity* (Philadelphia: Jewish Publication Society, 1976), p. 168.
9. Ibid., p. 100.
10. Ibid., p. 208.

manded its support. This would have invited an open confrontation between Federation and a major congregation—a situation no one relished. Yet many Federation leaders, not at all personally attuned to tradition and Halacha, could not appreciate the goals of the Chevra Kevod Hamet. The lack of community rabbinic support for the Chevra helped confirm the Federation leadership's negative response to the Chevra. Not insignificantly, many of these leaders were wealthy, and their own value system favored "more" rather than "less," even for funerals.

Given these factors, a sizable segment of Federation's leadership could hardly be expected to remain neutral on this issue. Community controversy was a concern, for fear that it would adversely affect the campaign. At the very least, there was the real possibility of lesser contributions from the heads of the Jewish-owned funeral home and their supporters if they felt "abandoned" by Federation.

Pressure, albeit "unofficially," was put upon Adath Jeshurun and upon me to reconsider the "Enga decision." The argument was that community unity had to be protected lest "the campaign be hurt." Federation's leadership showed little interest in evaluating the Chevra's impact upon the quality of Jewish life, nor was there any assessment of whether a community-wide discussion of funeral practices was valid. Federation's goal was a successful campaign before all else. Adath Jeshurun responded that it would stand by its "Enga decision."

Since synagogues in the Minneapolis community receive no Federation subvention, Adath Jeshurun could challenge Federation without concern for economic repercussions. Vis-à-vis the Federation, Adath Jeshurun was independent, and could therefore act in a manner consistent with the wishes of its membership. If it were a subventee, would it have been possible—or as easy—to maintain this independent posture? Most likely not.

The most recent controversy within the Minneapolis community is whether to honor the request of Temple Israel (a Reform congregation) for a subvention for its Hebrew school. The Conservative congregations, in opposing this request (for reasons growing out of both their ideology as well as of their assessment of what constitutes a true community educational program), have warned that if Temple Israel's request is honored, they, too, may request funding for their many educational programs.

Should this take place, the synagogues might well discover that they, too, have been brought into the Federation orbit and become subject to communal discipline as interpreted by Federation. This could compromise the independence of the synagogues and have a dire effect upon the synagogue's potential to be a major critic of Federation.

Elazar notes that linkage between federations and synagogues "has become one of the primary items on the American Jewish community's agenda for the coming years."[11] The rise of the large modern congregation, with "its voracious need for funds to sustain a multi-faceted program, has placed them in basically the same position as any other agency in the community."[12]

The caveat is clear: "Even with their [Federation's] general commitment to self-restraint in imposing their policies on constituent and recipient agencies, their extension of funding privileges has been accompanied, *quite properly,* by a demand on their part for some say in their programs."

Had Adath Jeshurun been a recipient of Federation funds, the latter's leaders could well have pressed for a review of a congregational program which Federation regarded, by its criteria, as harmful to the community.

The synagogue's role, quite properly, should be that of the

---

11. Ibid., p. 227.
12. Ibid., p. 293.

community prophet applying the values of the tradition in evaluating Federation's values and postures. Any one synagogue, in turn, will have to defend its own policies from the criticism of sister synagogues and the Jewish community at large. Ultimately, however, the community's Jewish character is best assured by synagogue independence.

In light of Federation's unofficial but real attempt to pressure Adath Jeshurun into terminating a program it regarded as a vital expression of Jewish tradition, Elazar's concluding sentences in *Community and Polity* are especially cogent.

> This process of more and more funding by Federation is not only likely to continue, but has probably been accelerated as a result of the Yom Kippur War [October 1973] and the funding agreement that emerged from it. Synagogues are already beginning to turn to Federations in search of support for their schools. This trend is likely to expand, and it may even be that Federation funding will find its way into other activities previously the preserve of the religious, congregational or any of the other activity spheres of American Jewry.[13]

The Synagogue and Unilateral Action

A major criticism of the Chevra grew out of its impact both upon the community and upon sister synagogues. There was no denying that each synagogue was an independent entity, with the power to do as it wished, but the question was raised whether any synagogue had the right to take unilateral action which affected the community and other congregations.

Elazar is correct that the synagogue is beyond community discipline. This, of course, does not endow it with the right to act irresponsibly, for there are values and guidelines which are incumbent upon every group which perceives itself as

---

13. Ibid., p. 377.

being within the community. The Jewish community, however, is not monolithic; subcommunities and special-interest groups abound within it. A synagogue is such a "subcommunity," with the right to establish its own models. It has the right to say to others in the community: "You needn't join us nor must you accept our pattern. If, however, you wish to learn from us or to adapt our program, feel free to do so."

It is counterproductive for the community to regard any and all controversy as detrimental to its best interests. Dissent is vital to develop community positions, provided that the dissent's purpose is to further community growth. If the community were to become a monolith, whose criteria would prevail? The rabbinic tradition that "controversies that are for the sake of Heaven will endure" is valid even today. Hillel may be normative, but Shammai is necessary to assure that the former will reflect a well-thought-through thesis.[14] Even as a group suffers if individual dissent is throttled, so must the overall community suffer if groups or subgroups within it are stifled—even for the sake of unity.

Whether the Chevra Kevod Hamet, or any project, will succeed or fail depends on whether it is perceived to have validity and value. There is little doubt that a significant percentage of the families served by established funeral homes are dissatisfied. It is also obvious that someone patronizing a Jewish-owned funeral home whose clientele reflects a wide variety of commitment, from Orthodox to Conservative to Reform, cannot automatically assume, unless specifically requested, that Halacha will be followed. Monopoly is always costly to the consumer, while competition tends to guarantee more value and greater satisfaction. Although Jews generally prefer to patronize Jews, there is no reason for Jews to restrict themselves to coreligionists, regard-

---

14. Hillel and Shammai, two first-century sages, were often in great disagreement. Although the majority embraced Hillel's position, Shammai's teaching served as a valuable foil in developing the norm.

less of price or quality of services, simply on the grounds of Jewish loyalty, any more than Gentiles should be encouraged to support only Gentile firms. (Jews know how threatening the Christian "Yellow Pages" were to Jewish merchants!)

The community dialogue on whether Twin Cities Jewry was best served by its continued exclusive patronage of the Jewish-owned funeral home was a positive contribution to community growth. Adath Jeshurun believed it to be legitimate and responsible to challenge the assumptions upon which community commitment to one funeral home was based. To seek to suppress the dialogue and the controversy on the grounds of unity is counterproductive.

The marketplace of ideas serves us well only if there be open traffic within it. While the community debate was never conducted in a forum with equal time for "pro" and "con," the many discussions in such informal settings as homes, cocktail parties, and synagogue social hours provided ample opportunity for the issue to be aired. In the process, the community was enriched, as it came to understand that there was now a valid and viable alternative available to families making funeral arrangements.

It would be wrong to assume that the entire Adath Jeshurun membership supported the Chevra. Many were unhappy with the congregation's policy of making death such a priority agenda item. Some were sensitive to the "unity" issue; they were convinced that dissent would lead to dissension. Some business people felt that the congregation, by offering a lower-priced "package," was competing unfairly with the Jewish-owned funeral home, which could not meet the Chevra's price.

The congregation board was sensitive to these feelings; each of these positions was, in fact, represented on the board, where floor debates on the Chevra—often heated—were not unusual. Some board members were very concerned that Adath Jeshurun was involved in the funeral business. This issue was sharply joined when the board debated whether the services of the Chevra should be extended to nonmember relatives of Adath Jeshurun members. The question was especially cogent where the *met* was an elderly parent who had possibly been institutionalized for many years, and, at death, was not a member of any congregation. The debate centered on whether the Chevra's goal was to serve the dead or the survivors. Should the Chevra turn its back on a member whose loved one is not a synagogue member?

The board's debates illustrate how far-reaching the Chevra program could become. The consensus was that the Chevra's services should be limited to members, although there was some discomfort that nonmember parents of members were being abandoned. Jewish law makes a definite distinction between mourning the death of a parent and of any other family member. *Kriah* is cut on the right side, except when one is mourning for a parent; then the cut is made on the left side over the heart. The *kaddish* period is thirty days, except when mourning the loss of a parent, when the requirement is for eleven months.

The board responded to this value system. Although the board felt it was not appropriate for the Chevra to handle nonmembers, because this somehow moved the congregation into the marketplace, yet parents were parents. A motion passed in January 1977 granted a six-month grace period in which nonmember parents could be served by the Chevra.

During that time members would be encouraged to continue the membership of elderly parents or, if they were unaffiliated, to enroll them in the congregation. Articles in the *Clarion* underscored synagogue membership as a link with life which should not be denied to elderly parents. This put the burden of serving parents where it most appropriately belonged—upon their children. In the process, the value of *kevod horim,* respect for parents, was introduced and taught. To date, some children have enrolled, or re-enrolled, their parents. More to the point, fewer elderly people are now being withdrawn from membership; a vital link with life has been increasingly sustained.

While the Chevra has not been embraced by the entire Adath Jeshurun membership, there have been no resignations as a result of this program. Families new to the Twin Cities and young people affiliating with a synagogue for the first time, however, have been attracted to Adath Jeshurun because of the Chevra. For the vast majority of the synagogue's members, the Chevra has been a source of pride; more and more they have come to appreciate its role within the congregation and the community.

The Funeral Industry

Paranoia seems to dominate the funeral industry whenever it is confronted by the allegations of its critics. The national Funeral Director Associations consistently respond aggressively to what they deem a threat to their business. Jewish funeral directors are, in this regard, no exception.

Although many critics of the Chevra sought to describe it as an economic response to high prices, the Chevra leadership has continuously maintained that it is not merely a memorial society interested in helping consumers save money. The Chevra's goal is to encourage a return to tradition, and the traditional model, being simple, tends to cost less. The Chevra correctly understood that an attack on the price structure would obscure the Halachic issues; it would direct the community debate into a consideration of whether or not prices were too high. There is, of course, no simple answer to that question since people's pocketbooks do differ.

Most critics of the funeral industry, however, continued to raise the economic question. The Synagogue Council report on funeral practices states that its purpose is to "present some remedial alternatives which could lead to the reassertion of Jewish communal control over Jewish funeral practices, toward the goal of making the Jewish funeral both *less costly* and more meaningful in accordance with Jewish tradition" (emphasis added).[15]

A member of the MRA inquired of Rabbi Solomon Freehof, a leading Halachic authority within the Reform rabbinate, whether it is permissible to utilize a Gentile undertaker when there is a Jewish one in the community. Rabbi Freehof in his response dealt with the economic question. He affirmed that there is no objection to a lower price and that a Gentile undertaker is not *treif* (ritually unacceptable) ab initio, although he cautioned that only Jews should handle the *met*. Freehof then urged that the Jewish undertaker be supported because of his special role in the community, in that he provides funerals for indigent Jews, contributes to Federation, is a member of synagogues, and so on.[16]

Freehof's defense of Jewish-owned funeral homes was raised in the Twin Cities and nationally. Since the Jewish-owned funeral home did assume, at some cost to itself, certain communal responsibilities, should it not be given the total support of the community? Few seemed interested in exploring an alternative to this economic argument by pointing out that we might all be better served financially if the Jewish community itself, through Federation funds, were to assume the cost of burying the indigent, thereby reducing the price of Jewish funerals. No one, in fact, seemed to really know how many indigent were buried free-of-charge or for a modest price.

The economic issue was raised by the Jewish-owned fu-

---

15. *Toward New Policies on Jewish Funeral Practice* (Washington, D.C.: Institute for Jewish Policy Planning and Research, Synagogue Council of America, Analysis no. 56, April 1976), p. 1.

16. Rabbi Freehof's response is included in his *New Reform Responsa* (Cincinnati: Hebrew Union College Press, 1980).

neral home in another guise. Its rationale for not agreeing to a lower price for a Chevra funeral was that this, in effect, would be a subsidy to Adath Jeshurun, and the cost of the subsidy would then be passed on to the other patrons of the home. Such a show of favoritism to Adath Jeshurun members would be patently unfair to the rest of the community.

Economic issues, once raised, take on their own character, and the Chevra wisely restrained itself from snapping at the bait. Over and again, it was made clear that the Chevra had not been created as an economic solution to the problem of high funeral costs. The Chevra's model of a funeral that was both Halachic and dignified was an attempt to involve people in the process of caring for the dead. Adath Jeshurun asserted that by caring for its own in death, it manifested the congregation's concern for its members while encouraging people to assume responsibility for one another.

The Jewish Funeral Directors Association (JFDA) entered the fray early and vigorously. It lost little time in labeling the Adath Jeshurun Chevra Kevod Hamet, its chairman, its members, and me as scoundrels, manipulators, do-gooders, and malicious people whose only goal was to take the bread out of the mouths of established business people. The JFDA continues to wage its war against the Chevra. In the Boston area, a major Jewish-owned mortuary has purchased a print of the ABC-produced documentary *A Plain Pine Box,* which it makes available to organizations. The film is brought by a mortuary representative who periodically halts the film to offer an ongoing critique of the Chevra. He then concludes with the blatantly false statement that the Chevra Kevod Hamet has failed. The volunteers aren't interested any more. It no longer exists at the Adath.

One of the early responses to the Chevra by the Jewish-owned funeral home was the contention that the Jewish mortician, because of his vast experience in dealing with families, is the true expert in Jewish funeral practices. The

Chevra representatives who originally met with the local Jewish funeral director were astounded to hear him contend that true Jewish tradition did not demand simplicity and that the authentic model was the one that preceded Rabbi Gamaliel.

Throughout the country, Jewish funeral directors have developed close personal relationships with rabbis, and the latter are generally content to deflect to the former as much responsibility as possible. Jewish funeral directors treat rabbis with great courtesy and take care of their every need: transportation, clergy rooms, and above all, the privilege of allowing the rabbi to determine the time of the funeral.

The Synagogue Council report offers its own explanation for rabbinic inertia where the funeral industry is concerned: "The fact is that local Rabbis regularly receive referrals to officiate at funerals in Jewish funeral establishments, and despite their distress at the situation, they may be unwilling to speak loudly to change the system."[17] Certainly in communities where most Jews are unaffiliated with synagogues, there are economic rewards to being one of the rabbis on call to conduct funerals for nonaffiliated families. Rabbis who serve in retirement communities can be kept as busy as they wish by the mortuaries. Yet even where there is no economic factor involved, there is a general apathy when it comes to challenging the monopoly of Jewish-owned funeral homes. As one rabbi in the Twin Cities remarked, "It's just comfortable dealing with someone who knows what I want done!"

The Chevra was accused by the local Jewish-owned funeral home of having maligned it. There is no question that the Chevra was—and is—critical of the Jewish-owned mortuary. The Chevra report is an "up-front" assessment of the professionalism that has monopolized an area in which people themselves should be more involved. The Jewish-owned

---

17. *Toward New Policies on Jewish Funeral Practice*, p. 4.

funeral home serves the public, and no one who serves the public can hope to please all the people all the time. Criticism in inevitable, and to dismiss it out of hand as malignment begs the issue.

The Adath Jeshurun Congregation refused to enter into a power struggle with the Jewish-owned funeral home of the Twin Cities. Congregation members who wish to patronize that establishment are free to so do; they are served, as always, by the Adath Jeshurun rabbi, cantor, and professional staff. At no time has the Chevra sought to interject itself into a private business. It has never asked to see the books, nor has it raised the issue of whether Jewish funerals are too costly.

The consumer is the best protector of his wallet. The Chevra's concern is but to legitimate and popularize the Halachic alternative.

6

The Medical Ethics Seminar

Does the concept of *kevod hamet* conflict with medical science? *Kevod hamet* requires that the body be treated with respect; that it be neither disfigured nor dismembered. Few Jews (or middle-class people generally) are prepared to donate their bodies to science (i.e., to become the cadavers dissected by medical students in their study of anatomy). The relevant question for most Jews is whether or not to consent to autopsies and organ transplantations. Do these procedures, which involve cutting the body, violate its "honor"? Is there a distinction between an autopsy and organ transplantation? What does Jewish law require, and how should the Chevra Kevod Hamet advise its congregation's members?

Autopsy was the first subject studied. It is not a new issue. Whether or not an autopsy violates *kevod hamet* has been debated by Halachic authorities for over two hundred years. Medical science insists that autopsies help broaden its horizons, and that the information gathered in a post-mortem examination frequently is of great help in treating other patients suffering from similar ailments. Where an autopsy literally helps keep another patient alive, the concept of *pikuach nefesh* (saving an endangered life) is invoked: the entire Torah may be suspended to help save even one life.

Although well aware of the principle of *pikuach nefesh*, traditionalists have been reluctant to permit autopsies. They would limit consent only to the situation where a patient

57

suffering from a similar disease is literally *l'fanenu* (before us) and could be directly helped by the information gleaned from an autopsy. Traditionalists, however, are not inclined to give *l'fanenu* so broad an interpretation as to grant automatic permission for an autopsy in every situation.

The consensus of Halachic authorities is to prohibit autopsies. Starting from that premise, the Chevra, dedicated to a Halachic model, decided to develop its own position on autopsies.

The Chevra's leaders believed it essential to explore both the Halachic and the moral implications of permitting—or denying—an autopsy. Thus the decision to create a medical ethics seminar. Dr. Roslyn Kaplan, a resident in pathology, agreed to serve as seminar chairperson. Her interest in autopsies was directly related to her professional activity and also to her mother's decision to authorize an autopsy when her father died but some months earlier. The conflict and pain created by his death and by the subsequent postmortem examination motivated Dr. Kaplan to join the Chevra. Medical people, attorneys, lay people, and rabbis were invited to participate in the seminar, which was projected as an ongoing study experience leading to position papers on a variety of medical ethics issues. In her letter inviting participation in the seminar, Dr. Kaplan wrote:

It is proposed that the first topic be limited to autopsy, as this is the issue most directly relating to the work of the Chevra Kevod Hamet. A preliminary agenda for study is as follows:

1. What is an autopsy? How, if at all, does it differ from desecration of the dead?
2. What are the origins of the Halacha regarding autopsy? Do the original sources address themselves specifically to the question of autopsy? If not, how does this affect a twentieth-century position?
3. If autopsies are permitted on the basis of *pikuach nefesh*, how do we distinguish between immediately saving a life,

potentially immediately saving a life, and remotely saving a life (i.e., the advancement of science)?

4. Should the Adath Jeshurun Chevra Kevod Hamet formulate a position on autopsy which it would then disseminate to both the congregation membership and the general public?

5. Assuming (4), should this position be used but for guidance or should it be a requirement for a family that wished to utilize the services of the Chevra?

6. If and when autopsies are permitted, what role should the Chevra play in influencing the autopsy process (e.g., draping of the body, surgical stitching of the incision, return of body fluids, retention of organs and fluids for research and further study, etc.)? Is this merely a Halachic issue or an ethical one as well?

While not every invitee accepted, a surprising number of people did join the group. Doctors, lawyers, accountants, a journalist, and a nurse were among those who participated in the seminar. Guest speakers were invited, and material was presented from Halachic, medical, and legal perspectives. Intense reactions to autopsies were shared as the nonmedical people learned what was actually involved in a post-mortem examination. There was increasing concern lest the seminar be "too generous" in permitting autopsies, and the consensus was that where they were permitted, some restrictions should be imposed upon the doctors.

In the United States, autopsies are expressly forbidden (except where required by a coroner) without written consent of the next of kin. Many seminar participants were uncomfortable with the fact that the standard permit form authorizes general, and unlimited, examination of the body, granting the pathologist the right to retain organs, fluids, and body parts deemed essential. There was concern that autopsies ofttimes are little more than "fishing expeditions," with the medical goal being but to add to the general body of knowledge. Members were also disturbed by the autopsy procedure. The body is stripped naked, placed on an examining table, cut open, examined, and then resewn. The stitching by the diener (the pathologist's assistant), often hurriedly done, tends to be sloppy, in no way conforming to the standards of the surgical stitch.

The writings of Jakobovits and Rosner were studied and debated.[1] A consensus slowly emerged: l'fanenu is a valid Halachic concept. Given today's rapid communication, information gathered in one part of the globe is quickly shared with medical colleagues the world over. L'fanenu can no longer be limited to helping only a patient who is in the same ward and of whose existence doctors are personally aware. The seminar concluded that autopsies are not inconsistent with Jewish law, but that certain cautionary steps should be taken.

The seminar then prepared a full report on autopsy, and following a vigorous debate, it was approved. This report also included a new authorization form which the seminar believed to be consistent with Halachic concerns. This form has been sent to all Twin Cities hospitals with the following explanatory statement:

> The problem is the need to carefully balance the need for autopsy as a life-saving procedure and the danger of autopsy becoming routine and hence disrespectful of the dead.
>
> The Medical Ethics Seminar of the Adath Jeshurun Chevra Kevod Hamet has proposed that an autopsy should be allowed and, in fact, may be required, but only when it is performed to obtain specific valuable medical information about a disease that can be utilized in the saving of lives of others who have contracted the same disease. However, the extent of the autopsy examination should be limited to the specific questions it seeks to answer, and it should be conducted with dignity and with respect.

---

1. Immanuel Jakobovits, *Jewish Medical Ethics* (New York: Bloch Publishing Co., 1975); Fred Rosner, *Modern Medicine and Jewish Law* (New York: Bloch Publishing Co., 1972).

The report and the form were the product of an interdisciplinary team effort, reflecting the contributions of many people, who had to exchange medical, legal, and Halachic concepts to arrive at a position.[2] This effort, inspired by the goal of developing a viable and relevant Halachic model, will hopefully inspire study of other issues where, through similar diligent interdisciplinary effort, Halacha can be given new relevance.

All too often, wrestling with Halacha occurs only in rabbinic circles. The laity, who also have real concerns and can make important contributions, are not involved, except as occasional consultants. Rabbinic-lay cooperation, with all participants sharing their expertise and with the final product a joint effort, can revitalize Jewish law. As the laity studies Halachic sources and grapples with their relevance, a greater loyalty and deeper respect for Halacha must develop. No one synagogue need feel it is inadequate to the task; all that is essential is a willingness on the part of rabbis and lay people to share with each other the subjects of their respective expertise.

Equally significant to the seminar debates was the discussion by the congregation's board of directors as they considered the report. The board received the text in advance of the meeting and had the opportunity to study it beforehand.

The debate was stimulating, and many board members expressed satisfaction that some of their time and energy was being spent on other than fiscal/administrative issues.

The seminar is now exploring organ transplantation. Is *kevod hamet* violated by allowing parts of the body to be cut away and used for another person? Among the issues raised are:

---

2. See Appendix 5.

1. Definition of death (since kidney and heart transplantations should be done immediately *prior* to death).
2. Is brain death a valid Halachic criterion?
3. Is there a difference between corneal transplants and kidney transplants?
4. Does it make a difference if the organ is taken with a specific donee in mind, or can an organ be taken to be placed in a bank for subsequent transplantation?
5. Can a person agree to be a live donor (usually of a kidney), although this might weaken him or her thereby creating the possibility of serious health complications?

Materials on these and other aspects of medical ethics have been published in Israel. The seminar is studying some of the Hebrew articles, albeit in translation. When a consensus emerges, the seminar will publish its second paper.

The seminar has become an ongoing study group, exploring ways to synthesize Torah, science, and law. The process itself has created greater respect for Halacha and its insights. As one member of the Chevra wrote: "The acting out and discussion of medical ethics is an appropriate response to the combination of burgeoning technology and slow-changing morality."

7

Chaverim

As the Chevra model evolved, it became apparent that procedures had to be developed to handle details normally attended to by the mortuary: writing the obituary and placing it in the newspaper, arranging for the grave opening, ascertaining who would be the pallbearers, guiding the family in completing forms for Social Security and veteran's benefits, and so on. These details are generally worked out during the family's prefuneral visit to the mortuary office. The workaday, businesslike, and impersonal setting at the mortuary strengthens the perception of the funeral arrangement as a commercial process, and this is what the Chevra has sought to change.

A team of people was recruited to assume the responsibility of meeting with the bereaved family to help them make the necessary arrangements. These volunteers were called *chaverim* (from the Hebrew *chaver:* "friend"). As designed, two *chaverim*, a man and a woman, serve the family as contact persons. They arrive soon after the death and remain "on call" to the bereaved during the hours preceding the funeral, at the funeral, and during the week of *shiva.* The *chaverim* also visit the family at the conclusion of the *shloshim,* the thirty-day mouring period following the death.

While a number of people agreed to be *chaverim*, they were, for the most part, apprehensive about their ability to interact with a family that had just become bereaved. How should they approach a grieving spouse or child or parent? What should they say? What would the family expect? Would the mourners be receptive? What should the *chaverim* do—or not do—in order to avoid offending the bereaved?

Chaverim candidates had questions about the details and paper work that are inevitably part of funeral arrangements. We live in "paper prisons," and there was some doubt whether the volunteer nonprofessional could become sufficiently knowledgeable to offer competent guidance and counsel. Which details could be handled by the *chaverim* and which should be channeled through Enga?

An in-service seminar was scheduled to deal with these concerns. For several hours one Sunday morning and afternoon the *chaverim* were taught by a panel of experts. A psychiatrist and a psychologist discussed the dynamics of grief to sensitize *chaverim* to the more common angry responses of the bereaved. Anger at times stems from frustration with God for His "harsh" decree, and at other times from guilt because "I didn't do enough or the right thing for papa." There is the rage which grows from a sense of abandonment because "my husband has left me knowing that I can never hope to manage." The *chaverim* were helped to understand that the anger was not their doing, and that they would be serving a positive function by allowing the bereaved to "vent."

The rabbinic presentation was built on the Halachic insight that "One speaks to the bereaved only about the dead." *Chaverim* were taught to open their interviews with the family by asking a direct question about the deceased: How long was she ill? Was it quick? Did he suffer? etc. The *chaverim* learned that such queries are not in poor taste; on the contrary, they give the family permission to speak. *Chaverim* were sensitized that only after there is some release of feelings can the family begin to deal with the specific arrangements.

The funeral director present at the seminar distributed

and discussed a checklist of items to be handled: how to contact the cemetery to arrange for a grave opening, the process in which the family might share in preparing the obituary, the information to be included, the guidance to help the family choose pallbearers, the manner in which the forms for various burial benefits (Social Security and VA) are best completed.[1] Since the coffin is part of the Chevra "package," this most vital aspect of the pre-funeral visit with the mortician was of no concern.

The entire in-service session was punctuated with questions, comments, and reactions. When it ended the *chaverim* had a sense of what was required of them, how they were to respond, and the support system that their rabbi and Enga would provide for them.

With each family served by the Chevra, the *chaverim* procedure took on more definite form. Upon learning of a death where the Chevra is called upon, I contact the *chaverim* team on duty. They, in turn, immediately contact the chairpeople of the Chevra Kadisha and the *shomrim*. The *chaverim* call the family to arrange for their visit. At times the *chaverim* precede my prefuneral visit; at times they come after. It seems to make little difference. Once with the family, the *chaverim* go through their checklist, but only after the family has been encouraged to talk about its loss.

The *chaverim* attend the funeral and then return to the *shiva* house to conduct a brief ceremony as a family member kindles the seven-day memorial candle. They visit during the week of *shiva* and call upon the family to mark the end of *shloshim*, the thirty-day mourning period.

At the funeral the *chaverim* organize and gather the pallbearers together so I can instruct them in their responsibilities.[2] Once at the cemetery, the *chaverim* join the cantor

---

1. See Appendix 6.
2. See Appendix 7.

and me in shoveling some earth into the grave, thereby setting an example for others at the burial.

Some concern was expressed about whether the *chaverim* might infringe upon the rabbinical role. Does their speaking to the family about *shiva* and explaining the Chevra model usurp the rabbi? Our experience has demonstrated the contrary, the *chaverim* underscore and affirm what the family hears from me. The repetition, in fact, often enables the mourners to comprehend more fully what I have said to them. Bereavement is a trauma, and mourners often find it difficult to focus fully, the first time, on what is being said. The repetition helps.

From a rabbinic perspective the assurance that the *chaverim* will handle most details makes it easier for me to devote full attention to helping people through the mourning process. There is also a powerful and positive impact in the fact that there are two lay members of the congregation who are volunteering a great deal of time to help. The reaction is: Somebody really cares; my synagogue really cares! This is significant for both family and congregation.

One major responsibility of the *chaverim* is to explain the Chevra model to the family. They must assure the mourners that the *met* has been taken to the mortuary and that the *tahara* has been—or will soon be—performed by the Chevra Kadisha. An effort is always made to recruit *shomrim* from among the family and friends of the *met*.[3] This not only fills in some of the time slots, but it involves the family, often grandchildren, nephews, nieces, in the process of showing *kevod* (respect) to a beloved member of the family. Such participation has positive effects. It sensitizes people to the reality of death, particularly to the death of someone cherished. A widow who learns that her grandchildren have been *shomrim*, or a daughter who observes that her chil-

---

3. See Chapter 8.

dren's friends are sitting *shemira* for her mother or father, feels strengthened and gratified.

The *chaverim* have come to play an important liaison role between the Chevra and the family. Mourners are far more comfortable when necessary arrangements and details are taken care of in their living room or den. This overcomes the negative impact of commercialization and the attendant sense of impersonalization about which so many mourners have complained. As the *chaverim* do their work, the family is comforted, reassured, and supported.

8

Shomrim

Traditionally, *kevod hamet* required that the *met* not be left alone between death and interment. At the very least, one person should serve as *shomer* (from the Hebrew: "to watch" or "to guard"). Often, *shemira* (watching) was done by one or two men who served the community as professional *shomrim* and were paid for their effort. Given the tradition of immediate burial, *shemira* seldom lasted as long as twenty-four hours.

In our modern mobile society, it is not unusual for funerals to be delayed forty-eight or even seventy-two hours in order to give a far-flung family time to assemble. This is one reason why *shemira* has been all but discontinued. As more and more responsibility was placed on the mortician and with less and less contact by the public with death, *shemira*, except among the very traditional, has come to be viewed as an anachronism. Jewish-owned mortuaries generally refrigerate the body, and usually no one, other than the mortuary staff, has any physical contact with the *met*.

The Chevra committed itself to restore the tradition of *shemira,* albeit vesting it with new form. In place of one or two "professional" *shomrim,* a team of people was enlisted to serve as a *chevra* of *shomrim,* a society of guardians. Men, women, and teenagers (sixteen and over) were invited to commit themselves in teams of two to "sit" *shemira* for a block of two hours. The twenty-four-hour period was divided into four six-hour periods, with a captain in charge of each quadrant.

The *chaverim* are responsible for contacting the appropriate *shomrim* captain in order that *shemira* begin as soon as possible. The captains of the other three quadrants are also alerted so that they can arrange for their assignments.

Shemira is an opportunity for people to reflect upon the meaning and purpose of life. Sitting in the presence of a *met, shomrim* are encouraged to meditate or to study. Historically, *shomrim* would read the Book of Psalms (in Yiddish, *zoggen tehillim*), the beloved book of religious poetry which has inspired generations of Jews. The Chevra's *shomrim* may read psalms or utilize any of the books made available for study and/or perusal. These include the Bible (with individual and annotated copies of the Books of Psalms and Job), meditational literature, volumes on death and dying (e.g., Kubler-Ross, Feifel, Reimer), and a variety of articles which are suitable reading for *shomrim*.

Inevitably there was a request to ritualize the *shemira* process. To meet this need, the following "Procedure for *Shomrim*" was developed:

1. The *shomer* (guardian) performs a true *chesed shel emet*—an act of selfless loving-kindness. The *shomer*'s role is to affirm that until the *met* is buried, *kevod hamet,* honor to the dead, demands that the *met* not be abandoned.

2. The *shomer* should utilize the time in the chapel to reflect and to meditate upon the meaning of life in general, and of his or her life, in particular.

3. For this purpose, a library of books and articles dealing with some aspect of death, dying, grief, etc., is available at the mortuary.

4. The *shomer* can choose to recite passages from the Psalms and other books of the Bible, or to read other library material.

5. The holiness of this task requires that there be no talking between the *shomrim* while in the *shemira* room. There is also to be no smoking, no eating, no drinking.

6. Try to arrive ten minutes before your shift begins. At the appropriate time, enter the *shemira* room. Recite the *Shema* standing, and after your predecessor has left, take his or her seat and utilize the time meditating, reciting, or reading.

7. When your relief appears, rise and recite the following prayer: (It will be available at the mortuary.)

My God, You have created the soul within me;
You have formed it. You breathed it unto me and you preserve it within me.
So long as my soul is within me, I acknowledge You, O Lord, My God and God of my ancestors, as Master of all creation.
I pray unto You, O Lord, who unites soul and body, that the soul of the *met,* whose body I now leave, will find rest in Your sheltering care.

Amen

Shemira volunteers reflect a broad cross-section of the congregation. Some retired members accept early-morning hours (midnight to 8:00 A.M.). College students seem to favor Saturday nights–Sunday mornings from 2:00 to 8:00 A.M. Many USY'ers (synagogue youth group members) have been rostered, as have a host of congregation members. Families previously served by the Chevra frequently express interest in helping others. For most people, *shemira* is their introduction to the Chevra.

An especially pressing problem arose when the Chevra had to deal with its first Shabbat (Sabbath) death. According to Halacha, the *met* is not to be moved until Shabbat ends (forty minutes after sunset). Arrangements have now been made with hospitals and nursing homes to allow the *met* to remain in the room where he or she died until Shabbat is over. On those occasions, *shomrim* have sat in hospitals, and often side by side with members of the family.

The vast majority of *shomrim* speak positively about the experience. One teenage participant wrote: "Looking back on my involvement in the Chevra, I see that it has served a purpose beyond what I had expected. Since I have participated in sitting *shemira* and reading extensively about death and dying, my perspective of death has changed drastically. . . . I have realized death as it is; that is, as a part of life; as important and inescapable as birth."

Shemira has been a valuable conduit through which to express love, care, and respect. The death of a beloved ninety-year-plus revered teacher brought forth an outpouring of *shemira* volunteers. More came forward than were needed. His students seemed to ache to perform this act of true righteousness for a man they loved.

In another instance, a bereaved daughter, entering the *shemira* room to sit for her own mother, had a glimpse of the full dimension of her life as she confronted her own friends who had volunteered to sit *shemira*.

Death is never pretty, yet the Jewish view that we dare not abandon the dead introduces us to the act of "true charity": doing for others without any thought of reward. In Judaism, this is the highest form of *mitzva*.

9

Chevra Kadisha

Tahara, the purification of the body through a prescribed ritual of washing, is the single most important ritual of preparing the *met* for burial. This final act of kindness to the dead is entrusted to the members of the Chevra Kadisha (lit. the Sacred Society). They are the last human beings to touch the *met;* they effect the final contact between the living and the dead.

Historically, every family had the responsibility to care for its own dead—including performing the *tahara.* Not unexpectedly, this task was naturally assumed by a small group of dedicated men and women, often on a professional basis. In most American Jewish communities, the Chevra Kadisha comprises a handful of men and women who share a deep commitment to Jewish tradition. The Chevra Kadisha generally performs the *tahara* on the premises of the mortuary—be it under Jewish or Gentile ownership. In communities served only by a Gentile-owned mortuary, it is the Chevra Kadisha which assures that the burial conforms to Jewish tradition.

Participating in a *tahara* requires courage since it involves handling the *met,* who must be raised, lowered, turned, combed, and washed. Where death was preceded by a serious illness or major surgery, the task is even more demanding; the *met* may not be a pretty sight.

The Chevra Kadisha has its parallels in other cultures which also place value on "laying out" the dead. Until the end of the nineteenth century, this was an accepted practice in rural America as first- and second-generation Americans continued with "old world" customs and traditions. Some communities, like the Amish, maintain their traditional practices to this day.[1] In its commitment to care physically for the dead, the Chevra Kadisha is neither unique nor strange.

Minneapolis is served by a community Chevra Kadisha, consisting of a small group of men and women—generally well-advanced in years. The lack of younger people in the community Chevra Kadisha is a serious concern. While the community Chevra Kadisha performs *tahara* on the premises of the Jewish-owned funeral home, its services must be specifically requested by the family. The mortuary generally negotiates with the Chevra Kadisha and also makes the preparation room available.

As the Chevra began to evolve, it decided to assume responsibility for total care of the *met*—including *tahara*. In part, there was the desire to offer families a full service; in part, there was concern that the community Chevra Kadisha, which had indicated that it would not perform *tahara* in a non-Jewish-owned mortuary, would be unavailable to us. The Jewish-owned mortuary, in fact, made it clear that it would not allow anyone to participate in a *tahara* on its premises if he or she were part of a team doing *tahara* in a Gentile-owned mortuary. The Chevra, having made the decision to create its own Chevra Kadisha, had to deal with the reality that with but one exception, not a single member of the Chevra had ever participated in a *tahara*.

Men and women were approached to explore their interest in performing this *chesed shel emet,* this act of true kindness. Those solicited included doctors and nurses. Little by little, twenty-two men—including me—and eighteen women

---

1. Kathleen B. Bryer, "The Amish Way of Death: A Study of Family Support Systems," *American Psychologist* 34, no. 3, pp. 255–261.

agreed to be part of the Chevra Kadisha. My decision to join the Chevra Kadisha flowed from my perception that the pace of the leader is the pace of the game. I sensed how vital it was for me to be a model.

Recruiting volunteers to join the Chevra Kadisha was but the first task. The process of developing a procedure was equally difficult. What rituals of purification would best reflect the ambience of Adath Jeshurun, a Conservative congregation? Careful study of various Chevra Kadisha rites affirmed that there was no single set of rituals or liturgies. Some procedures required that the deceased be held upright over straw; others placed the *met* on a board. Some dressed the *met* in *tachrichim* (shrouds), which included trousers, a long *kittel* (smock), and an appropriate head covering—a *kippah* (skullcap) for men and a bonnet for women. The men would be wrapped in a *tallit* (prayer shawl); women would have an apron tied around their waist.

An in-service study session for all Chevra Kadisha volunteers was held in June 1976. As rabbi, I presented basic Jewish sources, and a pathologist who had joined the Chevra Kadisha added vital medical insights.

The group learned about rigor mortis and also about the ease with which a dead body can be bruised. The body, therefore, was to be handled as little as possible. The *tahara* would be done with the *met* placed on a "prep" table with a tilt top; the head would be in the upper position so the water could run from head to toes and then into the drain.

There was a variety of prayers from which to choose. After much deliberation, texts describing various parts of the body were selected from the Song of Songs. These verses, in the original Hebrew and in English translation, were pasted on cards and enlarged to poster size, so they could be easily read while the *tahara* is performed.

Tachrichim would be a simple long gown with a cloth belt. Aprons would not be used for women (it was regarded as "sexist"), but a *tallit* would be used for men. An appropriate head covering would be used for both men and women.

The process requires six gallons of water (the equivalent of the traditional nine *kab*), which would be poured uninterruptedly, usually by two people.

When the in-service session ended, the Adath Jeshurun Chevra Kevod Hamet had decided upon its own *minhag* (custom). Its approach would reflect the values of a Conservative congregation committed to tradition.

In September of 1976, shortly before the Chevra was to become operational, the members of the Chevra Kadisha gathered for a second training session, this time at the Enga chapel. The purpose was to review the *tahara* procedure and to simulate the process upon a live volunteer. Tension was high as the group began to review the process and the prayers. Everyone knew that the next step was to enter the preparation room for the simulated *tahara*. This involved penetrating the "bowels" of the mortuary, and walking through rooms where caskets and other items would be in obvious view. Finally, there was the preparation room itself; many wondered how it would feel to stand where dead bodies had been "processed."

Following the study session, the group quietly—almost solemnly—walked through the mortuary. There was a hushed seriousness as the Chevra Kadisha surrounded the "prep" table and one of its members, clad in a bathing suit, climbed on the table. A team of five men then simulated the ritual. They hesitated, they made mistakes, but all in all, the group learned the process. As tension lessened, people became more secure in contemplating their service on the Chevra Kadisha.

Enga agreed to provide a storage cabinet for the various supplies necessary for *tahara:* buckets, towels, prayer cards, *kippot,* and rubber boots. Everything was in readiness for the first time the Chevra Kadisha would be summoned.

Everyone in the group reported experiencing the same irrational hope that they would never be needed. All knew that the first *tahara* would be difficult—even as it would be a moment of truth for the Chevra itself.

During the course of the following months, the Chevra Kadisha showed itself to be competent, available, and responsible. Whenever there was a death, a team of either five men or five women, on short notice, made themselves available.

The following *tahara* procedure was adopted by the Chevra Kevod Hamet.

1. Preceding *tahara* the team gathers in the mortuary's anteroom to review the procedure. The team captain assigns members their positions: head, shoulders, legs. The captain also tells his or her colleagues the Hebrew name of the *met,* and if the *met* is male, ascertains that the *tallit* is on hand.

2. The team silently files into the preparation room, proceeding to the cabinet to gather the necessary items for the *tahara.*

3. Once everything is in place, the team captain refers to the *met* by Hebrew name and asks to be forgiven for any indignity which may inadvertently be done to the *met* during the *tahara.*

4. With the prayer cards in place and three buckets of water filled, the sheet is removed from the *met.* With great care, the body is turned from side to side as water is poured over every part of the body, accompanied by the recital of the appropriate prayers in Hebrew and in English.

5. With the completion of the washing, the *met* is dressed in *tachrichim* (and *tallit*) and placed in the coffin. A bit of earth from *Eretz Yisrael* (the Land of Israel) is sprinkled over the body and *sheberlach* (shards) are placed

over the eyes. The coffin is closed and then wheeled to the *shemira* room.

The entire procedure takes forty-five minutes. Members of the Chevra, when asked why they "subject" themselves to this task, respond that for them this is the highest *mitzva*. They have the sense of accomplishment that comes from doing the right thing for its own sake. One member stated succinctly, "The *met*, like an infant, has to be taken care of. We try to handle him gently, in a caressing and comforting manner. He can do nothing for himself; we must do for him. I hope when my time comes, someone will do the same for me."

10

The Cemetery

Tradition, which exhorts direct participation in the burial as *kevod hamet,* also places importance on the site of the interment. In the Jewish value system a cemetery is more than a tract of land, it is a *beit-olam* (an eternal home). The cemetery is *kadosh* (holy) because human beings are there laid to rest. A visit to the graves of parents, grandparents, or dear ones is regarded as a pilgrimage to *kever avot* (lit. ancestral graves). Tombstones, historically, have long been an important source of information to students of any Jewish community.

The deep Jewish commitment to cemeteries has always targeted Jewish burial places, together with synagogues, for desecration during anti-Semitic uprisings. In Nazi Europe, thousands upon thousands of tombstones were overturned. From 1948 to 1967, when East Jerusalem was occupied by Jordan, the ancient Jewish cemetery on the Mount of Olives was desecrated; its tombstones were used to build army barracks and latrines.

The significance of the cemetery as a community institution is reflected in the well-nigh universal desire of Jews, even those with but a marginal Jewish identity, to be buried in a Jewish cemetery. Jewish cemeteries vary in their bylaws, but virtually all exclude Gentiles from burial in their midst.

For years, public policy in the United States has accepted that since cemeteries organized by religious and ethnic groups serve a productive and useful purpose, they are, deserving of tax-exempt status. When this policy was initiated, it was a sensible decision; the land utilized for burial was often on nonarable soil located on the outskirts of the community and unsuitable for any other purpose.

With the expansion of urban areas, cemeteries which were once far out suddenly occupied large parcels of expensive real estate in the midst of the city. Although most cemeteries are not really charitable associations, they have maintained their tax-exempt status, although not without challenge. Opponents have charged that cemeteries "are not organized for the purpose of providing a burial place for those who die insolvent, but to enable individuals to provide for themselves, or their families, a suitable place to be interred, upon payment of reasonable compensation."[1]

Cemeteries, during the past half-century, have accrued large reserves of capital, partially through pre-need sales, but in no small measure through excessive charges for opening and closing graves, for setting up stone monuments or bronze plaques, and for perpetual care. The last-named in particular, established as endowment funds to guarantee future care, are often quite substantial. Mitford insists that "more than one thousand cemeteries have perpetual care funds in excess of one hundred thousand dollars, and more than fifty cemeteries have funds in excess of one million dollars. All-in-all, the money held in such funds in the United States totals over one billion dollars."[2]

The public generally has no knowledge of who owns the cemeteries, unless it be a synagogue or some other charitable organization. In the latter instances, there may be some accountability, especially if the by-laws of the parent organization require reports from all committees.

Cemeteries owned by cemetery associations, however,

1. Jackson and Percival, *Law of Cadavers* (New York: Prentice-Hall, 1950), p. 292.

2. Jessica Mitford, *The American Way of Death* (New York: Simon & Schuster, 1978), p. 144.

enjoy almost total independence. Information regarding their affairs tends to remain a mystery. Given the natural hesitation to probe deeply into the affairs of institutions which handle the dead, cemeteries have come to enjoy a relatively free hand in dealing with the public.

Cemeteries seemingly function without being subject to state or local regulations. They make their own rules and formulate their own price structures. Each lot owner pays dearly for his small tract of land and also must assume a variety of ancillary costs, such as grave opening and closing, monument erection and perpetual care, with the sum total of these additional charges more than doubling the original purchase price. Within the cemetery gates, the cemetery superintendent interprets policy, often setting it on a moment's notice.

The three largest Jewish cemeteries in south Minneapolis illustrate this process. Each is owned and governed by a cemetery association. Their books are secret; and while their leaders make sparse and sporadic reports to the cemetery board, no information is shared with the general membership. The by-laws are not available, and the rules of operation are structured for the convenience of the cemetery rather than for the needs or the wishes of the public.

During the course of the years, these cemetery associations have developed an ongoing working relationship with the community's Jewish-owned mortuary. While there has been controversy as to who is to arrange and charge for the Chevra Kadisha or who is to sell the grave liner or vault, the mutual cooperation between mortuary and cemetery has generally been a boon to both parties. They are supportive of one another, and for good reason.

The emergence of the Adath Jeshurun Chevra Kevod Hamet caused real tension between the congregation and the cemetery associations. The latter were aware of the anger of the Jewish-owned mortuary and were unwilling to cooperate with a group viewed as an intruder. In addition, Enga was not known to Jewish cemetery personnel. The first families served by the Chevra were often victims of the cemetery's begrudging and slow response to the Chevra's request for a grave opening. There was also unpleasant harassment even at the burial service when the secretary of one of the cemetery associations threatened not to permit the burial without a "kosher" *tahara*. He challenged the Chevra's procedures as not conforming to Halachic standards. He also took to hovering about the grave in order to ascertain that everything was being done properly.

These obstacles were eventually overcome, in part because open controversy does not serve the purposes of cemetery associations, and in part because it soon became obvious that the Chevra's goal was not the dissolution of the cemetery associations.

As the Chevra developed, it explored ways to simplify and personalize the burial process, which today relies upon the use of graveside lowering devices. The popularity of heavy and ornate metal caskets led to the development of mechanical devices to lower the caskets into the grave. These devices turn slowly, and removing them is always a cumbersome process. After the casket is lowered, the cemetery maintenance crew must kneel in order to shimmy the device's straps from under the casket and roll them up. Following this the "track" and the board upon which the device has been wheeled into place must be removed. In order to save time and to end the uncomfortable wait during the casket's lowering and the removal of the device, the practice has developed of placing the casket on the lowering device and covering it with an artificial grass mat during the burial service. Following the recital of the *Kaddish*, everyone is directed back to the cars. Only then is the casket lowered and the grave filled.

The lowering device proved to be an obstacle to the Chevra's design of having family and friends share in filling the grave. Given the light wood coffin, the former practice of lowering the coffin by hand-held ropes presents no problem. It is, in fact, done with ease by the pallbearers and others close to the family. This return to tradition is, from the viewpoint of the Chevra, sensible and desirable.

Two of the three cemetery associations soon refused to permit the hand-lowering of the coffin. The Chevra was informed that the device had to be used "because of insurance." There was a concern, perhaps legitimate, that someone participating in the hand-lowering might slip, and in the event of an injury, hold the cemetery liable. Upon learning of this ban on hand-lowering, the Chevra chairperson wrote to the secretary of one of the cemeteries requesting a copy of the by-laws governing burial procedure. This request, to date, is yet to be honored.

Maurice Lamm reports that some cemeteries have a policy of prohibiting pallbearers even from carrying the casket from hearse to grave "because of the possible insurance hazard in case of accident while family members are carrying the casket." He concludes with the pious hope that "proper cemetery insurance coverage, however, takes into consideration the traditions of the Jewish people on a Jewish cemetery."[3]

Cemetery-association membership is vested in plot owners. The associations, as nonprofit corporations licensed by the state, are accountable to their members. Since Jewish cemeteries trade on Jewish loyalty, they should be accountable to the Jewish community and accommodate themselves to its needs. Practices based upon the requirements of Jewish law or the sensitivities of our tradition should be encouraged and not resisted.

Finances are another issue. Cemetery reserves—or a sub-

---

3. Maurice Lamm, *The Jewish Way in Death and Mourning* (New York: Jonathan David, 1969), p. 60.

stantial portion of them—should be used for appropriate communal purposes: Jewish education, support of *Torah* institutions, and so on. Should the association refuse to assume such responsibility, then given its healthy cash flow, it should reduce its fees and charges. The fact is that the public has little awareness of the cemeteries' financial situation. The handful of people in charge of a cemetery association succeed in keeping the finances secret because an apathetic public has refused to become involved. The Jewish community, like the public at large, resists grappling with the simple realities articulated by Jessica Mitford:

> Economies achieved by new and efficient operating methods, tax exemptions such as only schools and churches enjoy, dedication to "pious and public use"—these would all seem to point in the direction of continuously reducing the cost of burial. The opposite has been the case. The cost of burial has soared at a rate outstripping even the rise in undertakers' charges.[4]

In this inflationary era, as the funding for Jewish programs and projects becomes more and more difficult, it is appropriate to ask hard questions in order to direct the flow of public money into creative and life-enhancing projects.

---

4. Mitford, *The American Way of Death,* p. 125.

11

Rituals of Bereavement;
or, Memorial Cocktail Parties and *Shiva*

Lynne Caine's book, *Widow*, was one of the catalysts that lead to the study which resulted in the Chevra Kevod Hamet. Together with the FTC report on alleged funeral abuses, *Widow* motivated my decision to utilize the 1975 Rosh Hashana sermon to call for a congregational committee to explore funeral and grief practices.

Ms. Caine describes how her husband, Martin, lapsed into a coma while hospitalized in the National Institute for Health (NIH) facility in Baltimore. Since he was no longer aware of her presence, Ms. Caine followed the advice of the doctors to return home to New York to be with her two children, Jon and Buffy. Ten days later, she was notified by phone that Martin had died. Although his death was imminent, Ms. Caine reports how the reality of the event numbed her.

She had already arranged with a local mortician to fulfill Martin's wish that he be cremated, with the ashes remaining in Baltimore. What was to be significant was the memorial service scheduled for New York in which a small group of family and friends would come together to share in Martin's loss.

The service was brief. A friend delivered the eulogy. Everyone then returned to her apartment. It seemed like a good idea because she desperately needed to be with people. She expected "that we would sit there, subdued, talking about Martin, wiping away a few tears, being tender, thoughtful, mourning him. But it was not like that at all. It was an enormous cocktail party."[1]

She found herself emptying ashtrays while exhorting her children to quiet down and to be well behaved.

> And I kept asking myself, "What am I doing here? Why am I talking? And laughing? What am I laughing at?" Then it dawned on me that I wasn't laughing. My guests were all having a good time and I was out of it. I was left out. . .
>
> I can't remember anything after that, but one of my friends told me, "You said, 'I'm tired and I'm going to bed enjoy yourselves.' And then you disappeared."[2]

The memorial cocktail party was overwhelmingly sad. People returned to Lynne Caine's home with the good intentions of strengthening a widowed friend during her travail, but the gathering was transformed into a celebration. Her friends, as they drank and smoked, seemed to lose touch with the purpose of their presence in the Caine home. This is markedly different from the Jewish tradition of *shiva,* where for a seven-day period the mourners "sit" at one home, to receive condolence visits by family and friends.

The laws of *shiva* are clear. The first assumption is that there are no guests in a house of *shiva.* Since the death of any person diminishes all humankind, everyone is a mourner. Callers at a *shiva* house dare not perceive themselves as coming to eat, drink, or socialize. Their purpose is to strengthen and comfort the mourners, who, in turn, are expected to devote their energy to mourning. Mourners are to do no work; they are not even to prepare their own meals.

---

1. Lynne Caine, *Widow,* (New York, Bantam Books, 1974), p. 56.
2. Ibid., p. 57.

This task is the responsibility of family, friends, or neighbors. The mourners must sit, literally; in some communities, they sit on the floor, and in others they sit on low stools or benches. An accepted modern practice is for mourners to sit on sofas or chairs from which the cushions have been removed.

Callers are not to speak to the mourner unless he or she speaks first; the mourner's right of silence must be respected! Should conversation begin, it should be about the *met*. The *shiva* call is an appropriate time for a caller to share a memory, a reflection, an experience which helps bring the *met* into clearer focus. A *shiva* house is not the place for general socialization, and visitors are urged to limit their stay.

The caller, upon leaving, traditionally does not say good-bye or *shalom,* for there can be no peace in the mourner's heart. A simple verse is to be recited: "May the Almighty comfort you even as He comforts all who mourn in Zion and in Jerusalem."

Although the mourner sits alone, overwhelmed by sorrow, the affirmation that he or she is part of a community is a source of strength. *Ma'ariv* (the evening prayer service) is a major group activity in a *shiva* house. In many communities mourners are encouraged to worship mornings at the synagogue, with the evening service conducted in the *shiva* house. The service, or *minyan* (from the Hebrew: "quorum"), requiring ten people, provides an opportunity for the mourner to recite the *Kaddish,* thereby proclaiming, in the presence of the community, his or her faith in God and in His decree. The *minyan* in the home has the effect of moving the synagogue into the mourner's living room.

The rules of *shiva* are simple. The word is from the Hebrew for "seven," since the mourners are to "sit" for a week—with the day of burial regarded as the first day, and with the "sitting" on the seventh or last day limited to but an hour in the morning. In celebration of Shabbat, mourners are forbidden to sit *shiva* from sunset Friday to sunset Saturday.

Psychologists and sociologists who studied the seven-day *shiva* period underscore its validity. Grieving is a process, and *shiva* provides the mourner with time to adjust to the trauma of separation and bereavement. Where an entire family sits *shiva* together, a natural setting is created in which it is possible to review the past, to settle accounts, and hopefully to resolve to develop a new set of meaningful relationships, albeit without the *met.*

Since this process takes time, Jewish law forbids the mourner to work, to shop, or to leave the *shiva* house (except to attend synagogue services). Traditionally, the mourner during *shiva* does not pay excessive attention to his or her personal appearance and, except on Shabbat, is to wear the rent garment or ribbon.

On the morning of the seventh day, however, the mourner must terminate *shiva* and return to his or her tasks. A short walk out of doors symbolizes the tradition's insistence that the living are to go on living.

The Halachic model is strikingly different from the scene Lynne Caine describes in *Widow.* Had she been part of a traditional Jewish community, Martin, of course, would not have been cremated. His body would have been returned to New York, for a funeral service which would have culminated in a cemetery interment. The family would then have come home for a simple meal, which would have included eggs (symbolizing life) and garbanzo beans (chick-peas). The mourners would have been served by others, who would have implored them to eat because the living must go on living.

Prior to the meal, a special seven-day memorial candle—a symbol that the human soul is a candle of the Lord—would have been kindled.

Somber reflection, however, makes the Jewish traditionalist painfully aware that the Halachic model is no longer the norm in every instance. In many a *shiva* home, the mood is precisely that of the memorial cocktail party; large trays of food and an open bar create an atmosphere inconsistent with mourning. Often pastries, coffee, tea—and even liquor—are served to the callers. The laden table inevitably results in a crowded *shiva* house as people linger and socialize over a second or third cup of coffee. Many Jews, knowing nothing of the traditional model, have come to regard this open-house atmosphere as the *shiva* norm. They, in turn, have pushed for a reduction of *shiva* to three nights or less. Within the Reform community, the three-day *shiva* is almost universal.

As the Chevra model unfolded, it was apparent that part of our task was to develop an awareness of *shiva* and of its potentially positive effect upon a grieving family. *Chaverim* reinforced my suggestion that nothing—absolutely nothing—be served to callers during the week of *shiva*. This helped alter the pattern of people overstaying and socializing. The family was also informed of the expectation that they were to "sit" for seven days. Only pressing matters, such as the impossibility of staying away from job, office, or store, might absolve the mourner from the religious obligation of sitting the full *shiva* week. The Chevra, in interpreting *shiva* along with other facets of the traditional model, has come to fulfill a vital educational role. The constant reiteration of the tradition's expectations and demands helps guide the bereaved in their painful confrontation with death.

12

From *Shiva* On

Shiva, when fully observed, is an intense experience. During the week many callers pay condolence calls and the mourners expend time and energy relating to people visiting them. Then on the seventh day, *shiva* ends and the house is suddenly empty of visitors. The days following *shiva* are, for many mourners, the most difficult period. Jewish law prescribes a less intense mourning process, known as *shloshim* (Hebrew: "thirty"), through the thirtieth day following burial. This is a time when the mourner is allowed—nay, expected—to return to a normal schedule, while yet observing some rituals of grieving such as not having a hair cut, or attending musical performances. When mourning the loss of a parent, the period is extended through twelve months following burial.

After *shiva,* however, mourners are on their own. Halacha does not legislate any specific role for the community to become a support system. It is apparent, nonetheless, that more often than not, the loneliness and disorientation which characterize bereavement do not end with *shiva.* The mourners still require an infrastructure to support them through an experience that continues to be intensely painful.

Joyce Phipps, in *Death's Single Privacy,* records some of her first-year experiences as a widow. Over and again her message is clear. As a bereaved widow, she was by and large left to her own resources. Although some friends and acquaintances demonstrated sensitivity and expressed concern, she still had to work through her grief on her own. Being blessed with religious faith, having a place within her church, and involving herself at a university in a master's program, she was able to create order in her life. But it was not easy. Joyce Phipps reports similar struggles of other widows and widowers with whom she joined in various support groups. She contends, and with no small measure of bitterness, that few institutions adequately serve widows and widowers.

Most singles groups and widow-to-widow programs fail, thereby intensifying the sense of loss, the feelings of bitterness, and the sinking sense of loneliness.

Halacha, unfortunately, is not without its own lacuna in this area. There are no *mitzvot* calling upon the community to support the bereaved during the post-*shiva* period. Even the Chevra, which marks the conclusion of *shloshim* with a visit from the *chaverim,* has not been sensitive to this challenge. With resignation and bitterness, Joyce Phipps criticizes "the clergy who do not follow up after the first week because they are too caught up in the pressures of administering their parishes."[1]

> The clergy and the laity of the churches expect the intensely grieving to exhibit different forms of social behavior. If the newly widowed do not come to church or drop out of social groups, then it is because "they just can't face people" and the Congregation responds by isolating them further![2]

> For most clergy, the demands of their day-to-day parish activities simply do not allow them the time required for follow-up on any one particular bereaved person. There is also the temptation to assume that a person in grief who *needs* help, advice or just moral support for what he/she is doing, will *ask* the clergy to provide such. Many of the clergy respond just like "ordinary"

---

1. Joyce Phipps, *Death's Single Privacy* (New York: Seabury Press, 1974), p. 124.
2. Ibid., p. 125.

people, who presume that once the grieving party has stopped looking as haggard as before or has begun to enter the world, in no matter how automated a fashion, the grief is ended.[3]

Jews loyal to the tradition of reciting *Kaddish* the year of mourning are strengthened by fellow worshippers with whom they participate in weekday and Shabbat services. The other worshippers often serve as a support group in which people can work through their feelings by relating to others who have undergone similar experiences.

Since most mourners, sadly, no longer follow the traditional practice of reciting *Kaddish,* it is essential to develop new post-*shiva* rituals to structure a process whereby members of a congregational community can reach out to the bereaved. The Chevra, which has succeeded in dealing with death and the early stages of grief, must now motivate itself to meet this new challenge of providing support from *shiva* on.

---

3. Ibid., p. 117.

13

The *Yahrzeit:*

Marking a Special Anniversary

It is a venerable Jewish tradition to observe the *yahrzeit,* the anniversary of a beloved's death. There is little, if anything, the living can do for the dead other than to remember them. The anniversary of a death is an appropriate occasion to pause, however briefly, for an expression of quasi-mourning. Specifically, this involves kindling a memorial candle at home (a one-day candle, rather than the seven-day variety kept burning during *shiva*) and attending services to recite the *Kaddish.* In most synagogues an appropriate memorial prayer can be recited, with some congregations commemorating the *yahrzeit* and reciting the memorial prayer on the Friday night either before or after the actual midweek date. Regardless of the form and specifics of the observance, the act of remembering enables people to maintain a sense of continuity with their dead.

Many may not be punctilious in observing the *yahrzeit* of a sibling, but children usually commemorate the anniversary of a parent's death. Most faithful in their *yahrzeit* observance are widows, widowers, and parents bereaved of a child. Of them all, widows who have not remarried are most consistent in their observance; they perform the *yahrzeit* rituals with a deep sense of commitment.

Joyce Phipps vividly describes the anxiety which gripped her as the first anniversary of her husband's death drew closer. Wanting desperately to be with people, she managed to have herself and her two sons invited by friends to dinner. The anniversary day was made even more painful when no one, other than one widowed friend, remembered, or cared, to call. The latter was particularly sensitive; she engaged Joyce in a long talk. "As she left . . . she said, 'Happy new year!' That's right, I thought. It is a new year. It was incredible what that statement came to mean to me as I ruminated with friends about the year . . ."[1]

Even if Joyce Phipps were Jewish and deeply involved in her congregation, chances are that no one would have reached out to her on that first anniversary. She would have received a synagogue notification reminding her of the *yahrzeit,* but this would have been a routinized impersonal card or letter. Joyce Phipps's feelings are undoubtedly not atypical: they cry for new rituals or practices. These, however, must involve others in addition to the rabbi, not because rabbis are unfeeling, incompetent, or uncomfortable with death. It is just that rabbis are involved in so many programs, projects, and activities that they have little time and energy to develop new areas of service which would extend them even further.

The Chevra has demonstrated that lay people can be competent, and that given the opportunity they will involve themselves. A rabbi, in a true spirit of lay-rabbinic collegiality, might organize a cadre of sensitive and concerned people to help him develop an appropriate support system and procedure for that first *yahrzeit* and possibly for subsequent ones as well. Even people who may not feel the need for support would be pleased to receive expressions of care and concern.

---

1. Joyce Phipps, *Death's Single Privacy* (New York: Seabury Press, 1974), p. 142.

This process, once begun, hopefully might enable widows, widowers, and bereaved parents to join in self-help programs which would be more than just discussion groups, as worthwhile as these may be.

The Chevra Kevod Hamet has as its motto: "To honor the dead; to strengthen the living." It should be apparent that the living must be strengthened well past the day when they rise up from *shiva*.

14

National Reactions

Maurice Lamm's primary goal in writing *The Jewish Way in Death and Mourning* was to gather into one readable volume all the Halacha on the subject. He intended it as a guidebook to help Jews interested in understanding and following a Halachic model. As of August 1979, 60,000 copies, an extraordinary run for a book of this type, had already been sold.

Lamm reports his ongoing amazement at the responses to his book. Letters from home and abroad continue to pour in. The work, apparently responds to a deeply felt need for support when confronting death.

There has in fact been an explosive interest in death during the past decade and-a-half. It is a serious subject gnawing at people's hearts. New books on death reflect the ongoing research in this field. This doesn't necessarily mean however, that it is any easier for people to accept the reality of death.

Eric Bermann argues that death has now become dysfunctional.[1] We find it difficult to focus on it, much less to come to grips with it. Knowing we cannot conquer death, we are anxiety-stricken by its inevitability. This, in large part, is due to our rejection of a belief in some form of afterlife and to the corresponding empty feeling that with death our exis-

---

1. Eric Bermann, *Scapegoat: The Impact of Death* (Ann Arbor: University of Michigan Press, 1973).

tence comes to an end. This, of course, helps to explain why Lamm's book, with its religious perspective on death, has become so popular.

If Bermann and other writers are correct, we now confront a two-edged phenomenon: We have become more open in dealing with death, but at the same time, we are discomfited by it and find it difficult to define its contemporary meaning. The response to the Chevra has been no less amazing than the response to Lamm. Whether as a consumerism issue or as an interest in the phenomenon of death or as a desire to demystify the process of handling the dead, inquiries continue to pour into the congregation. These have been motivated by stories published in newspapers, as well as by the ABC-TV production, *A Plain Pine Box.* This interest was totally unexpected, and it undoubtedly reflects the desire to acquire insight on confronting death. There is an apparent hunger in our society, among Jews and Gentiles alike, to learn how to return to a more traditional posture toward death. As social sensitivity develops and deepens, models such as the Chevra will become even more significant. Informed responses, social and individual, toward death will inevitably lead to new and more caring responses to two populations closest to death: the elderly and people stricken with life-threatening diseases.

The Chevra is not the only answer or the only model. We dare not, however, cavalierly dismiss the issues raised by the Chevra. Burial practices pose a profound challenge to all who would set Jewish tradition as a viable alternative before American Jews. If community leaders fail to deal with the issues raised by the Chevra, the community itself must seize opportunities to express its needs and demand that its leaders be responsible and responsive.

15

Epilogue

In an article published as recently as December 1979, Rabbi Marc Liebhaber continued to dismiss the Chevra while praising the services provided by the Twin Cities Jewish-owned mortuary. He referred to a "Congregation experiment offering funerals through a newly organized society," contending that with each passing year the Chevra served fewer and fewer families.[1]

Esther Katz, the congregation's president, succinctly stated the case for the Chevra in her response to Rabbi Liebhaber, citing the actual figures that nine families were served in the first year, eleven in the second, and ten in the third. She observed that "We do not measure success in numbers. What we do deem important is that we have responded to a need within our Congregation. We have fulfilled that need through involvement and with simplicity and dignity."[2]

Tom Wexler, the Chevra chairman, noted the impact of national interest in the work of the Chevra.

> ABC television produced a one-half hour documentary on the Chevra, and we have furnished copies of it and of other Chevra material to Jewish and non-Jewish congregations all over the United States. The time is right for involvement. . . .

1. *American Jewish World* (Minneapolis), December 21, 1979, p. 2.
2. Ibid., December 28, 1979, p. 4.

Life presents us with opportunities to extend our friendship. The death of a loved one is one of the most important opportunities. That's where the Chevra is at.[3]

The vast majority of the community will continue to follow the conventional process and turn to a mortuary to make all the arrangements for burial. The marketplace is affected, however, to the extent that more and more people no longer view a simple funeral as a disrespectful statement about the dead.

The Chevra's most pervasive influence is, perhaps, upon the people who involve themselves in the process. Following the death of a beloved aunt, a Chevra volunteer wrote me:

Death often thrusts to the front those things which rest within the periphery of our vision. Aunt Bessie's death afforded me the opportunity to see that which you had explored at High Holiday Services, viz., congregants who could act on a pararabbinic level. Because of my and my family's involvement in the synagogue throughout these past years, we were able to function intelligently within Jewish law and custom. Not only were we able to perform comfortably and knowledgeably, but we were also able to teach and create situations for others to experience and respond. Because I wanted *shemira* for my aunt, I called upon several relatives to join me in this practice and several of them did and indicated their appreciation afterward. Filling in the grave, a totally alien custom to my relatives, was opted for by many, and all of those who did it found it worthwhile. And once *shiva* began, I had daughters who could lead a service, enabling my mother and her sisters to recite the *Kaddish*. We were able to perform simply because we have been involved in the ongoing worship and learning opportunities that the synagogue and you have offered throughout the years.

This is not to say that we didn't need a rabbi, for we did. What it is to say is that you have given us the ability to act as free and independent people, a holy people, because of the Jewish knowledge we have accumulated.

Once again, thank you.

---

3. Ibid., p. 4, 6.

APPENDICES

Appendix 1

REPORT TO THE BOARD OF DIRECTORS
ADATH JESHURUN CONGREGATION

From: The Death and Mourning Practices Committee

The full committee met first on October 29, 1975, and has continued to meet on a regular monthly basis as follows: November 17, 1975, December 8, 1975, January 12, 1976, February 9, 1976, March 8, 1976, and April 5, 1976. In addition, subcommittees with specific tasks met during the interim periods between full committee meetings.

At the October 29th meeting, areas for investigation were agreed upon. They included:

1. To study Halachic and Rabbinic traditions in death, funeral, and mourning practices.
2. To provide a vehicle for pre-planning for death, including funeral arrangements and *shiva* procedures.
3. To re-educate Jews about legitimate options open to them based on Jewish and secular law.
4. To ensure continuation of specific Jewish funeral traditions, particularly the Chevra Kadisha.
5. To protect the bereaved at the time of their loss from undue emotional and financial pressures.
6. To produce a funeral and mourning practices manual that will guide the reader in following traditional

Jewish funeral and mourning practices as well as informal social and community practices.

7. To consider training a Chevra of death and mourning volunteer counselors.
8. To re-educate Jews about their right to die as a Jew.
9. To clarify cemetery procedures and practices.
10. To develop vehicles to sensitize the Congregation to properly respond to the crisis of death.

In subsequent meetings, the committee received reports on Minnesota laws regarding funeral practices and regulations, Rabbinic law on death and dying, the United States Federal Trade Commission investigation of funeral industry practices, and the work and meaning of the Chevra Kadisha, Holy Society.

Over the months, the committee's knowledge of Jewish and secular laws on death increased. The committee also achieved a thorough understanding of funeral and burial practices in the Minneapolis–St. Paul Jewish community. Out of this knowledge base, the objectives of the committee developed. They were three in number:

1. To develop an organizational structure within the Adath Jeshurun that could offer its membership an opportunity for a traditional Jewish funeral.
2. To develop a manual that would contain information and directions on traditional Jewish death, burial and mourning practices.
3. To develop an educational program that would inform the membership on the traditions in Jewish death and mourning practices.

These objectives were approved by the full committee. Subcommittees were then set up to propose a structure for an Adath burial society and an outline for an informational manual. The educational program plan was scheduled for later committee work.

The results of the Death and Mourning Practices Committee work are contained in the following two proposals:

1. To establish Chevra Kevod Hamet Society to honor the dead. (Details follow.)
2. To print and distribute to the membership the *Adath Jeshurun Guide to Traditional Death and Mourning Practices*. (Details follow.)

Chevra Kevod Hamet

Chevra Kevod Hamet (CKH) is a memorial burial society officially established by the Adath Jeshurun Board of Directors to serve members of the Congregational family who desire and agree to a traditional Jewish funeral as described in the following paragraphs. The services of CKH are available to all families in the Adath Jeshurun Congregation. Use of the Chevra's services is on a strictly voluntary basis.

A traditional funeral is one which honors the *met* (deceased) with a simple but dignified burial. It requires no ostentatiousness to impress the living, but it is rather a process that preserves the beauty and honesty of the life that has ended. In committing ourselves to a simple but dignified burial, we honor the dead and sanctify the name of God.

In accordance with guidelines established by the Rabbinical Assembly Commission on Law and Standards, the Chevra Kevod Hamet follows these traditional burial procedures:

1. The *met* is prepared for burial through the traditional process of *tahara* (purification) by members of the Con-

gregation who are constituted as a Chevra Kadisha. *Tahara* is washing of the body. The *met* is not embalmed.

2. The Chevra Kadisha dresses the *met* in the traditional burial garment called *tachrichim.*

3. CKH provides a plain wood *aron* (coffin) in which the *met* is placed for burial. Once the *met* is placed in the coffin, it will be covered and the body will not be disturbed or viewed.

4. The funeral service is conducted by the Rabbi and the Cantor of the Congregation either at the funeral chapel, the Synagogue or the cemetery in accordance with the wishes of the family.

5. The interment is in a grave without a vault. Before the *kaddish* is recited, the coffin is lowered into the ground and covered by earth. Friends and family of the *met* who wish to take part in the mitzva of burying the dead are encouraged to share in this sacred task.

The work of the Chevra Kevod Hamet is carried out by fellow-members of the Congregation. They are volunteers who have received special training to serve the families of the Synagogue. The CKH volunteers will

1. serve as members of the Chevra Kadisha,

2. sew the *tachrichim,*

3. construct the *aron,*

4. coordinate arrangements for the funeral and be available to help the family afterwards,

5. counsel with the family on the purchase of a cemetery plot, if needed,

6. assist the Rabbi in helping the family prepare for the traditional practice of *shiva.* This seven-day period of mourning, which begins on the day of burial, has deep religious and emotional benefit for the bereaved family.

Chevra Kevod Hamet will assist the family in making burial arrangements as follows:

1. We will arrange for the funeral director, who will effect all transfers of the *met*.
2. Our Chevra Kadisha will perform *tahara*.
3. We will provide the *aron* and the *tachrichim*.
4. We will call on the family and help make arrangements for the Synagogue, or chapel and/or graveside services.
5. We will provide transportation for the immediate family and the *met* on the day of the funeral.
6. We will advise the family, if necessary, on the purchase of a cemetery plot.
7. We will assist the family in writing the obituary and death notices.
8. A Chevra Kevod Hamet counselor will be available to the family through the period of *shiva*.

A Service to the Members of the Congregation to Honor the Dead

The services of Chevra Kevod Hamet are available to all members of the Adath Jeshurun Congregation. This means there will be no cost to the family for:

1. the services of the funeral director,
2. the services of the Chevra Kadisha, including the *tachrichim*,
3. the *aron* (simple wood coffin),
4. the chapel and graveside services or the services of the Rabbi and the Cantor, and
5. transportation for the *met* and the immediate family on the day of the funeral.

The cost of interment, including the plot, preparation and care of the gravesite, and the stone are the sole responsibility of the family and not of Chevra Kevod Hamet.

Chevra Kevod Hamet operates without fee to those it serves. The sole sources of funds are Social Security burial benefits, veteran burial benefits (if any), and tax deductible contributions.

Contact with Chevra Kevod Hamet can be made any time during a person's lifetime merely by calling the Synagogue office. A CKH counselor will help make all arrangements so that when a death occurs, the process described will be initiated. Arrangements can also be made when a death is imminent or after it has occurred. A member of the family may call the Synagogue office, the Rabbi, the Cantor, or the Executive Director. A CKH counselor will then be assigned to make necessary arrangements.

It is the intent of this Adath Jeshurun Congregation to offer a simple, dignified, and traditional funeral to its members. To accomplish this intent, the Chevra Kevod Hamet has been established to serve the living by honoring the dead.

Financial Support

1. The Death and Mourning Practices Committee proposes that the Adath Jeshurun Board of Directors award a one-time only grant of two thousand five hundred dollars ($2,500.00) to begin the work of Chevra Kevod Hamet. This money will be used to print the manual and cover the costs of initial start-up work and purchase of materials to construct *aronot* and sew *tachrichim.*
2. No further financial support will be needed from the Board. Social Security, veterans' death benefits and contributions will sustain CKH.

Organizational Support

1. The Death and Mourning Practices Committee rec-

ommends that it be established as a permanent standing Committee in the Congregational structure.

2. The Committee's function will be to operate Chevra Kevod Hamet, establishing its rules and monitoring its procedures.

In conclusion, CKH will begin training and preparing for its sacred work immediately following endorsement by the Adath Board of Directors.

Respectfully submitted,
DR. ALAN S. BRISKIN,
Chairman, Death and Mourning
Practices Committee

Appendix 2

EXPRESSION OF GUIDANCE
to
CHEVRA KEVOD HAMET of ADATH JESHURUN CONGREGATION
Minneapolis, Minnesota

This document is a guide for the family and friends of the deceased. It is not a binding agreement and may be revoked.

In the event of the death of _____
(Name of Person to be served by
Chevra Kevod Hamet)

the Rabbis, Cantor, Executive Director, or Synagogue Staff should notify the Chevra Kevod Hamet (CKH) that the family wishes to have the *met* honored with the services of CKH. A CKH counselor will contact the family immediately and begin assisting them in making funeral and burial arrangements.

Chevra Kevod Hamet agrees to honor the deceased with the following services without cost to the family: (1) We will arrange for the funeral director, who will effect all transfers of the *met* (body); (2) Our Chevra Kadisha will perform *tahara* (purification); (3) We will provide the *aron* (coffin) and the *tachrichim* (burial garment); (4) We will call on the family and help make arrangements for the Synagogue, chapel, and/or graveside services; (5) We will provide transportation for the immediate family, if needed, and for the *met* on the day of the funeral; (6) We will advise the family, if necessary, on the purchase of a cemetery lot; (7) We will assist the family in writing the obituary and death notices; (8) A Chevra Kevod Hamet counselor will be available to the family through the period of *shiva*.

The Family agrees to these traditional Jewish practices: (1) The *met* will be prepared for burial through the traditional process of *tahara* by members of the Congregation who are constituted as a Chevra Kadisha. *Tahara* is washing of the body. The *met* is not embalmed or cosmetized; (2) The Chevra Kadisha will dress the *met* in the traditional burial garment called *tachrichim;* (3) CKH will provide a plain but dignified wood *aron* in which the *met* is placed for burial. Once the *met* is placed in the coffin, it will be covered and the body will not be disturbed or viewed; (4) From the completion of *tahara* to the funeral service, the traditional practice of *shemira* (guarding the *met*) will be done by volunteer *shomrim* (guards) from the Congregation and, if possible, by relatives outside of the immediate family of the deceased; (5) The funeral service will be conducted by the Rabbi and the Cantor of the Congregation either at the funeral chapel, the Synagogue or the cemetery in accordance with the wishes of the family; (6) The interment will be in a grave without a vault. Before the *kaddish* is recited, the *aron* will be lowered into the ground and covered by earth. Friends and family of the *met* who wish to take part in the mitzva of burying the *met* will be encouraged to share in this sacred task.

Please complete one copy of the *Expression of Guidance* for each member of the family who will be honored by the Chevra Kevod Hamet upon his/her death. The Synagogue office staff will duplicate this document and send a copy to each person listed, to the Rabbi, keep one for the Synagogue file, and send one to be kept with your important papers. For further information call Rabbi Goodman, the Synagogue office, or any member of the Chevra Kevod Hamet. Shalom.

Enter the names of those family members, friends, and others who will take responsibility for advising the Synagogue that the deceased will be honored by the Chevra Kevod Hamet. PLEASE TYPE OR PRINT CLEARLY.

Name	Name
Address	Address
City, State, Zip	City, State, Zip
Name	Name
Address	Address
City, State, Zip	City, State, Zip

TO GUIDE MY FAMILY

In the event of my death, I_____, advise my family to call on the Adath Jeshurun Chevra Kevod Hamet to handle all necessary arrangements. I have read the list of services on this form provided by the Chevra Kevod Hamet and the obligations expected of my family and these conform to my wishes.

Signature of Person preparing this form   Date

Witness

Appendix 3

STATEMENT ON FUNERAL PRACTICE OF THE MINNESOTA RABBINICAL ASSOCIATION

Adopted by Minnesota Rabbinical Association, whose membership consists of Orthodox, Conservative, and Reform Rabbis:

Judaism teaches the equality of all men before God, the sanctity of human life, the dignity of the human personality, as well as the sanctity of the human body. The attitude of the Jew towards death and the funeral service manifests these noble doctrines of our faith.

Our religion demands respect for and consideration of man, in life and in death, and for his earthly remains. Judaism calls for understanding, sympathy and thoughtfulness in expressing consolation to the bereaved.

Our tradition commands that humility and simplicity be the rule and guide for all in the performance of the sacred last rites. Judaism maintains that these principles are to be expressed in acts of true loving kindness.

In keeping with these principles, the Minnesota Rabbinical Association recommends the following Jewish funeral practices:

1. Jewish funeral practice calls for a plain coffin. Expensive caskets are in conflict with the simplicity, humility, and equality demanded by Judaism.
2. The casket should remain closed to the public. Even the

109

family is not required to visit the mortuary prior to the funeral. Pre-funeral chapel visitation and reviewal of the body by the public are contrary to Jewish tradition and must not be practiced.

4. It is a Mitzvah to attend the funeral service and to join the funeral procession to the cemetery.

5. It is the tradition for the mourners to partake of a "Meal of Condolence" upon their return from the burial service. This meal should be provided for them by relatives and friends. This is not to be a social occasion. Elaborate food and drinks should be avoided.

6. It is a Mitzvah to visit the bereaved during the *shiva* period. Such visitation should be with understanding and compassion and should not become burdensome to the mourners. The purpose of this visit is not to socialize, but to comfort the mourners.

In addition to these practices, there are other customs and traditions to be followed in time of bereavement. For guidance in these matters, your rabbi should be consulted.

Appendix 4

RESOLUTION OF THE MINNESOTA RABBINICAL ASSOCIATION

Passed March 21, 1977

In the light of many misconceptions which recently have been created in our community, we, the rabbis of the Minnesota Rabbinical Association feel the responsibility to clarify our position with regard to Jewish funeral practices in the Twin Cities.

It has been our experience for several decades that in matters of funeral practices Jewish tradition to a great degree has been respected according to our individual rabbinic interpretations and requests. We appreciate that for decades Jews, regardless of circumstances, have been served.

We are fortunate to have the services of a Jewish mortuary in our community which has performed these services and has helped us maintain and carry out our responsibilities relating to Kevod Hamet (Care and respect for the dead).

In order to continue in this tradition, it is imperative to maintain a Jewish funeral home in our community. It is our conviction that such a policy is beneficial to Jewish communal life.

In order to insure the continued viability of such a policy, we call upon the Jewish Funeral Home in the Twin Cities to continue and intensify its positive response to the increasing

111

sensitivity and awareness of the teachings of our tradition as evoked by the Adath Jeshurun Congregational Chevrah Kevod Hamet, and to follow an economic policy that truly reflects the needs and the financial circumstance of every individual Jew.

Appendix 5

ADATH JESHURUN CONGREGATION
CHEVRA KEVOD HAMET
AUTHORIZATION FOR AUTOPSY

The undersigned, being the _____
                                    (relationship)

of the deceased, and being responsible by law for the duty of
burial, does authorize _____
                                    (name)

Hospital to perform an autopsy on the body of the deceased
_____ subject to such qualifica-
          (name)

tions as set forth below.

In consideration of the family's religious convictions and
in accordance with interpretation of Jewish tradition, permission is granted for autopsy on the grounds of acquiring
scientific information not apparent during life and essential
for the diagnosis and treatment of other patients afflicted by
a similar illness or disease.

Specify reasons for the autopsy: (To be completed by the
physician(s) requesting autopsy consent)

Specify restrictions and limitations:

The autopsy and incision(s) should be as limited as possible as is consistent with obtaining this information. Organs and fluids removed from the body must be returned for burial except for the minute amounts necessary for microscopic and laboratory studies. Organs may not be removed from the body if an "in situ" examination provides the necessary information. Further, the autopsy must be performed in a manner respectful to the body. This includes a respectful environment and conduct of personnel. Also, the body must be handled carefully, draped appropriately and all incision(s) must be properly sutured.

The body, together with all organs, tissues and body fluids will be returned for burial no later than _____

_____.

(Time and Date)

The physicians seeking the autopsy consent and the physicians conducting the autopsy shall be responsible for communicating the results in a reasonable period of time.

The undersigned reserve the right to have a designated medical representative of the Chevra Kevod Hamet present during the performance of this autopsy.

Authorized Signature(s) and Relationship:

Name of physician requesting consent:

_____

_____

_____

Name of pathologist performing autopsy:

Date and Time:_____   _____

Witness(es):

_____

_____

In those few instances where it is deemed necessary to retain temporarily one or more organs, permission is hereby granted, provided those organs are returned for burial as soon as possible.

Specify organ(s) retained and reason(s) for retention:

The organ(s) shall be returned for burial no later than

_____
                    (Time and Date)

Authorized Signature(s) and   Pathologist:
Relationship:

_____   _____

_____

Appendix 6

CHAVERIM CHECKLIST

RABBI'S RESPONSIBILITIES

1. Rabbi or Synagogue office receives an initial call and inquiries as to the wishes of the family con-concerning Chevra Kevod Hamet. The Rabbi secures the deceased's Hebrew name and conveys same to the counselor. _____
2. The Rabbi determines the precise time of the funeral and makes arrangements with Enga as to the time, the name of the cemetery, the location of the funeral service. After time arrangements have been negotiated, the Rabbi calls the family to confirm the time. Depending on the anticipated size of the funeral, determination should be made as to whether the funeral will be at the Synagogue, Enga, or the graveside. _____
3. Rabbi or Synagogue office calls the *Chaverim* on duty, and also notifies the CKH Chairperson _____
4. Rabbi explains *shomrim* and *shiva* to the family at initial visit. _____
5. Rabbi explains *kriah*. _____

CHAVERIM RESPONSIBILITIES

1. Immediately inform the leaders of the *Chevra Kadisha* that there has been a death. Call the

116

shemira captains. Ask to be informed when *she-mira* and *tahara* will commence. Remind the *Chevra Kadisha* Chairperson to notify the *shemira* coordinators when *tahara* will be performed so that *shemira* will not be scheduled at that time. ____

2. Call on the family and explain how Chevra Kevod Hamet functions. Leave the selected books which are part of the kit. ____

3. Fill in the death certificate—use Yellow form in calling information in to Enga, or arrange to make an appointment and drive by Enga offices to deliver information. All spaces must be filled in. Use such words as "unknown," "not applicable," as necessary. ____

4. Autopsy—All *Chaverim* should be familiar with "Expression of Guidance on Autopsy" from the Medical Ethics Seminar. Should the question of an autopsy arise, procedures are fully explained in the Expression of Guidance—if the *Chaverim* are asked questions re autopsy, please share this information in the report with the family. Also keep Rabbi Goodman involved. Upon completion, send one copy to Adath Jeshurun Synagogue. ____

5. Determine how many copies of death certificate are needed ($2.00 per copy). Suggest ten to twelve copies, as needed for Veteran's Benefits, Social Security, bank accounts, attorney, safe deposit boxes, etc. ____

6. Explain death benefits that may be available, such as Social Security or Veteran's Benefits. Obtain Social Security number. Social Security assignment should be made either to the spouse of the deceased or to the Chevra Kevod Hamet. It should be noted that a "B" after a Social Security

number means no death benefits are available for
the deceased.   ____

7. Fill out the necessary information for obituary
   notice (see sheet in kit for instructions). The
   following should be the standardized ending for
   every obituary notice: Arrangements made by
   Enga Memorial Chapels and the Adath Jeshurun
   Chevra Kevod Hamet. Obituary notices are $1.75
   per line, Minneapolis Star and Tribune; $1.00
   per line, St. Paul Dispatch. Deadlines for calling
   in obituary notices to newspapers are 10:30 a.m.
   and 5:30 p.m. Information to Enga half hour
   earlier at latest. Find out how many times the
   family wants the notice to run. Place obit notice in
   Jewish World (332-6318); call in on Monday
   morning for Friday issues in Jewish World.   ____

8. By law all information items 1–19 plus information on left side of yellow obituary and information sheet *MUST BE COMPLETED*. Enga uses
   this information to fill out death certificates and is
   required by law to submit death certificates to the
   Health Department within 5 days of death. They
   therefore need COMPLETE information as soon
   as possible, or no later than 2 days after death. ____

9. Call Enga with obituary information and confirm
   time of funeral and the opening and closing of
   grave. Determine whether the service is to be at
   Enga's, the Synagogue or graveside, depending
   on size of funeral. No funerals before 1:00 on
   Sundays at Enga. This call should be made before
   leaving the house of mourning, or else make an
   appointment to stop at Enga with this information.   ____

10. Give Enga instructions to type a clergy card.
    They should also be given instructions to bring

shiva candle and a box of acknowledgment cards
to the funeral and give to the *Chaverim* on duty.   _____

11. Clarify location of Enga—35 W and Diamond
Lake Road. Explain that the Rabbi has sensitized
Enga, and they are fully prepared to participate
in a traditional Jewish funeral.   _____

12. If funeral is at Enga, *Chaverim* should be
thoroughly familiar with the location of the various
rooms, including the family room. *Chaverim*
should be at the location of the funeral service
forty-five minutes ahead of time when there is a
large funeral to assist in ushering and directing
the family.   _____

13. Explain to the family the procedures for the day
of the funeral, including time of the limousine
pick-up and the procedures to follow at the
Synagogue, the Enga Chapel, and the cemetery.
If at the Synagogue, family will be taken to Fink
Room prior to funeral service and after funeral
service. The same procedures for Enga—family
goes to Family Room.   _____

14. Be sure the family understands *shiva* and inquire
if they will need assistance from the Chevra
Kevod Hamet to form a *minyan* for *shiva*. If so,
please call Shiva Chairperson.   _____

15. Explain to the family that in lieu of flowers,
contributions to the Adath Jeshurun Chevra
Kevod Hamet would be appreciated.   _____

16. Explain to the family re: contacting attorneys.   _____

17. Request the family's participation in *shemira;* ask
family to please assist with the *shomer* responsibilities, if possible, by asking for names of non–
immediate family members or friends to participate as *shomrim.* This is to be particularly em-
phasized if there is a long *shemira* period, such as

over a *Shabbat*. Also, ask family if they would serve as *shomrim* at other funerals at some future time. Call *shomrim* Chairpersons. ___

18. Explain billing for extras: Obituary notice, limousine (time and place of pick-up to be determined), death certificate copies, cemetery lot, grave opening and closing, police escort, and if there is a large procession, *use two escorts*. ___

19. Please request of the family that they keep their phone open for the next hour or so after *Chaverim* depart so that any additional information that is needed for the obituary can be obtained. On *Shabbat,* call the obituary notice in to Enga Director. Do not write. ___

20. *Chaverim* should arrange for the opening and closing of the grave. This should be double-checked with cemetery superintendent. Cemetery arrangement calls should not be made from the home of mourners. ___

21. Must have cemetery information, grave plot number and block number. Inquire whether charges for plot have been paid; if not, inquire as to who should be billed. ___

22. Ask about *Tallit* of the deceased (male) for burial with the *met.* Deliver or arrange to have it delivered to the Enga Chapel on Diamond Lake Road or to the *Chevra Kadisha* leader. Ask the family if they have some soil from Israel for burial with the *met.* ___

23. Arrange with family for 6–8 pallbearers. They may be male or female. Leave pallbearer instruction cards with the family. Explain procedure of lowering *aron* manually with the assistance of family or pallbearers at cemetery. ___

24. Ushering: The Executive Director of Adath will

be in charge of ushering when service is at the Synagogue. The Enga directors will be in charge when service is at their chapel. If funeral is at Adath, *Chaverim* should pick up Registry Books and give to family.   ____

25. The *Chaverim* should introduce themselves to the Enga director immediately upon arriving at the Synagogue, the chapel or the graveside.   ____

26. *Chaverim* will attend funeral and cemetery services and come back to the house and leave *shiva* candle and acknowledgment cards. *Shiva* candle should be lit with family in attendance. The prayer for *shiva* candle is as follows: The flame of the Lord is the soul of the man. *Ner Ado-nai nishmat adam.* We light this lamp in memory of ____.   ____

27. Cut out obituary notices and mail with *yellow form to Enga and* Synagogue.   ____

28. Call Chevra Kevod financial secretary re any funeral extras.   ____

29. A return visit should be paid to the family after the thirty days of mourning are up. At this time, the assignment of Social Security should be explained, and the Social Security assignment should be made to Enga. At this time, the bill for the extras should be given to the family. Families wishing to make a contribution to the Chevra should be encouraged in this decision.

ENGA RESPONSIBILITIES

1. Call the newspaper with the obituary notice.   ____

2. Call the cemetery re: Opening and closing of grave (see information on previous pages).   ____

3. Arrange for transportation of the *met* from the place of death to Enga.   ____

4. Send death certificate to the physician, etc.   ___

5. Fill in information on the clergyman's card. Bring *shiva* candle and acknowledgment card and give to *Chaverim* at the funeral.   ·   ___

6. Check, follow-up and assure that all essential arrangements have been made. Call Rabbi Goodman or the *Chaverim* if there are any problems.   ___

7. Be in charge of ushering and directing traffic if funeral service is held at Enga Mortuary.   ___

8. At the Synagogue, the director should feel free to assist the counselor or other appointed ushers. He should also feel free to instruct the pallbearers about their responsibilities.   ___

9. After the service at the Synagogue, the Enga Director *is in charge.* He will direct the pallbearers to the exit.   ___

10. The Enga Director will have responsibility for starting the procession after the family is in their cars and a reasonable number of other cars have been flagged.   ___

Appendix 7

INSTRUCTIONS FOR PALLBEARERS

To be honored as a pallbearer is to be given the privilege to fulfill the special *mitzva* of *l'vayat hamet* (escorting the deceased to the final resting place).

Pallbearers may also share in the final act of kindness, honor and love for the deceased—the actual burial. You may wish to help the Rabbi and the Cantor to fill the grave by shoveling some earth into it. This is a dignified and solemn act. You will be instructed in this process by the Rabbi, prior to the funeral.

As a pallbearer, please be at the place of the funeral twenty minutes before the scheduled service time. The Rabbi and a member of the Enga professional staff will visit with you prior to the service to indicate where you are to sit during the service, how to escort the coffin from the place of service into the hearse and what is expected of you upon arriving at the cemetery.

On behalf of the family and of the Chevra Kevod Hamet of Adath Jeshurun Congregation, we express our gratitude to you for your willingness to share in the *mitzva* of escorting the *met* to its final resting place, and for helping to strengthen the bereaved family.